Collins

Happy Handwriting

Teacher's Guide 5

> In their habitat, lions need cover like long grass or bushes in order to hide and stalk their prey. They also need water to drink.

> In their habitat, lions need cover like long grass or bushes in order to hide and stalk their prey. They also need water to drink.

Series Editor: Dr Jane Medwell
Author: Annabel Gray

William Collins' dream of knowledge for all began with the publication of his first book in 1819.
A self-educated mill worker, he not only enriched millions of lives, but also founded a flourishing publishing house. Today, staying true to this spirit, Collins books are packed with inspiration, innovation and practical expertise.
They place you at the centre of a world of possibility and give you exactly what you need to explore it.

Collins. Freedom to teach.

Published by Collins
An imprint of HarperCollins*Publishers*
The News Building, 1 London Bridge Street, London, SE1 9GF, UK

HarperCollins*Publishers*
1st Floor, Watermarque Building, Ringsend Road, Dublin 4, Ireland

Browse the complete Collins catalogue at
collins.co.uk

© HarperCollins*Publishers* Limited 2022

10 9 8 7 6 5 4 3 2 1

ISBN 978-0-00-848577-1

All rights reserved. No part of this publication may be reproduced, stored in a retrieval system, or transmitted in any form by any means, electronic, mechanical, photocopying, recording or otherwise, without the prior written permission of the Publisher or a licence permitting restricted copying in the United Kingdom issued by the Copyright Licensing Agency Ltd, 5th Floor, Shackleton House, 4 Battle Bridge Lane, London SE1 2HX.

British Library Cataloguing-in-Publication Data
A catalogue record for this publication is available from the British Library.

Series editor: Dr Jane Medwell
Author (lesson plans): Annabel Gray
Expert reviewer: Dr Mellissa Prunty
Publisher: Lizzie Catford
Product manager: Sarah Thomas
Project manager: Jayne Jarvis
Development editor: Abbie Rushton
Copyeditor: Alice Harman
Proofreader: Oriel Square Ltd.

Additional Practice sheet design template and icons: Sarah-Leigh Wills at Happydesigner
Cover designer: Sarah-Leigh Wills at Happydesigner
Illustrations: Jouve India Pvt. Ltd.
Typesetter: Jouve India Pvt. Ltd.
Production controller: Alhady Ali

Printed and bound in the UK using 100% renewable electricity at CPI Group (UK) Ltd.

MIX
Paper from responsible sources
FSC™ C007454

This book is produced from independently certified FSC™ paper to ensure responsible forest management. For more information visit:
www.harpercollins.co.uk/green

Contents

Handwriting: an important aspect of the modern curriculum	4
The *Happy Handwriting* course	6
Writing a school handwriting policy	8
Handwriting in the National Curriculum for Upper Key Stage 2	10
The teaching focus for each week (Year 5)	11
Letter formations	12
Teaching handwriting in Year 5	13
Teaching the *Happy Handwriting* lessons	15
Lesson plans: Units 1–10	17
Lesson plans: Units 11–20	27
Lesson plans: Units 21–30	37
Additional practice sheets	47
Assessing handwriting in Year 5	62
Handwriting example record sheet	66
Assessment record sheet for Year 5 handwriting	67
Assessment record sheet for joins in Year 5	68
Diagnostic assessment of handwriting sheet	69
Speed and fluency practice sheets	70
Extra practice sheet: diagonal joins	73
Extra practice sheet: horizontal joins	74
Extra practice sheet: joins to round letters	75
Extra practice sheet: capital letters for proper nouns	76
Guidance for alphabetical order tasks	77
Four-line writing guidelines: larger	78
Four-line writing guidelines: smaller	79

Handwriting: an important aspect of the modern curriculum

Handwriting that is efficient, fluent and readable is the basis of successful writing – it allows children to compose what they want to say. Handwriting is not only a medium through which much of the curriculum is learned; it also helps children to learn a range of important aspects of the curriculum:

- In the early years, the link between handwriting of letters and phonics embeds phonological knowledge.
- Efficient and automatic letter production contributes to the quality of what is written. Handwriting has been called 'language by hand'.
- As children get older, handwriting helps them learn the patterns of morphemes and letters, which are the basis of effective spelling.
- Learning to use a 'range of hands' lets writers allocate attention to activities like note-making, drafting and high-quality presentation.
- Looking critically at their own handwriting enables children to identify strengths and weaknesses, and improve their presentation.
- When handwriting is well established, older writers may develop their own style, as part of their academic identity.

Efficient handwriting is the foundation of learning in school and all children are entitled to be taught how to write effectively and legibly. *Happy Handwriting* offers children a carefully designed route to efficient, effective handwriting, using the simplest possible pathway.

Happy Handwriting

The content and structure of *Happy Handwriting* are based on a wide range of research into handwriting conducted around the world. This emphasises that direct teaching of a carefully structured handwriting programme is the best way to ensure that children learn automatic handwriting as efficiently as possible.

Evidence from handwriting research emphasises the importance of consistency and continuity in handwriting teaching. *Happy Handwriting* is a carefully developed progression from correct letter movements and joins in Key Stage 1, to consolidation of joins, size and spacing in Years 3 and 4.

In Upper Key Stage 2, *Happy Handwriting* promotes the consolidation of difficult joins, placing and spacing of letters and punctuation marks, aspects of proofreading and the development of personal style. Throughout Key Stage 2, *Happy Handwriting* develops children's abilities to write at different speeds depending on the writing task, so that they can learn to make decisions about when to prioritise neatness or speed, but always aim for legibility. These skills need regular, direct teaching and practice, which is presented in the children's books, slideshow presentations, this Teacher's Guide and the planning for each week. These resources build consistency and clarity in lessons and also help children to develop effective learning routines.

Not all children will learn with the same level of ease or at the same rate. It is important for both children and teachers to make assessments of the key aspects of handwriting progress and offer targeted practice to consolidate skills. In Years 5 and 6, children who struggle with automatic letter production or joining may find that their handwriting hinders their access to the curriculum or inhibits composition. *Happy Handwriting* provides appropriate assessment points, diagnostic materials and record sheets for teachers to identify children who need more support, and also offers additional practice materials.

Happy Handwriting provides teaching and practice materials but also asks you to assess handwriting outside handwriting lessons, as this is the ultimate criterion for successful learning of handwriting.

Key principles of Happy Handwriting

- *Happy Handwriting* sees handwriting as 'language by hand' and recognises that efficient, automatic letter generation contributes to the quality of what children write.
- *Happy Handwriting* teaches a simple, modern cursive font with exit strokes (or flicks) from the very start, to prepare the children for efficient joined handwriting. You can use this font to prepare materials or displays for children, or to make additional worksheets.
- *Happy Handwriting* is a planned, cumulative programme of skills teaching that involves regular review and assessment, so that teaching can be adjusted to meet children's needs.
- *Happy Handwriting* teaches the correct letter movement for each letter right from the start. This is the most effective way to develop a 'hand habit' that prepares for joined handwriting.
- If children learn the correct letter movement as a 'hand habit', it will become automatic, so that they do not need to allocate cognitive attention to it. In reading, we aim for all children to learn sound–symbol correspondences to the point where they are automatic, and in writing we want children to produce letter movements automatically. This takes practice, so *Happy Handwriting* provides the materials to practise handwriting 'little and often' and encourages parents and carers to help children do small amounts of practice at home.
- *Happy Handwriting* teaches efficient joins between letters as early as possible.
- Adult handwriting joins letters for efficient writing, but adult handwriting does not join every letter. *Happy Handwriting* teaches joined handwriting using the efficient joins but does not join 'break' letters, as that reduces writing efficiency.
- In Years 5 and 6, *Happy Handwriting* teaches children to write quickly and legibly, so that they can choose when to prioritise speed in their writing.
- In Years 5 and 6, *Happy Handwriting* offers diagnostic assessment materials to facilitate the identification of children who will benefit from using the additional resources in this Teacher's Guide and printable resources. In this way, the needs of individuals and groups can be addressed.
- *Happy Handwriting* teaches letter names and alphabetical order so that you can talk about lower-case and capital letters, as well as spelling, and introduce children to resources such as dictionaries.
- *Happy Handwriting* introduces proofreading to older writers, to build good writing habits.
- *Happy Handwriting* promotes the efficient use of resources to maximise teaching time and support teachers' preparation and assessment.

The *Happy Handwriting* course

Happy Handwriting provides guidance and resources for you to teach efficient, fluent and legible handwriting as simply as possible, and to create a clear, shared handwriting policy in school. *Happy Handwriting* teaches the key elements of early handwriting – letter movements, alphabet knowledge, joins between letters and well-proportioned writing – as early and thoroughly as possible. The course then supports writing at different speeds and with different attention to neatness, depending on the circumstances. Finally, *Happy Handwriting* promotes the development of an efficient personal style of writing.

Handwriting should be taught specifically, and separately from phonics or spelling instruction. However, letter formation and knowledge of letter names contribute to phonics and literacy learning. Children who can form letters correctly and automatically, and can discuss the letters by their names, can use these skills in their spelling and writing. The teaching of correct letter movements early in children's literacy learning is an important foundation of fluent and automatic handwriting. By Years 5 and 6, all children should know the letter names and alphabetical order. If any children struggle with these, it is not too late to intervene and improve their performance, which will help with simple tasks such as dictionary use, as well as with their handwriting.

In Years 5 and 6, most children will have learned the correct movements for letters and the main joins used in *Happy Handwriting*. They will need to practise controlling the size and relative proportions of letters, and learn to make the trickier joins between letters automatically and smoothly. They will also learn to make choices about when to 'speed up' their writing, with the inevitable trade-off for neatness, while retaining legibility. In Years 5 and 6, *Happy Handwriting* addresses printing in lower-case letters and capitals, when appropriate.

Some children will find learning handwriting relatively easy and a few may almost seem to 'catch' it effortlessly. However, other children will find handwriting challenging and need more practice and attention. *Happy Handwriting* builds in regular teacher assessment and self-review of handwriting by children, and you can use the additional resources to identify and support children who need more guided practice. There is assessment advice and a record sheet for handwriting assessments for each family of letter movements, and printable materials for home activities to support children's handwriting development. Short bursts of practice at home can be very effective, especially when supervised by an adult or sibling.

Letter formation is a movement, not just a shape

There is a letter formation movement in *Happy Handwriting* for each letter. It is very important that children use this movement every time they write the letter, always starting in the right place. Learning the letter movements automatically is the basis of fluent handwriting that does not demand cognitive attention from writers. On the sheet of letter formations, the dot is the starting point and each arrow represents a directional stroke. These are set out on page 12 of this guide so that you can identify any children who are inconsistent in their letter formation.

For children who know all the letter movements automatically, the relative height of letters is the next priority. In Key Stage 2, children should use an exercise book or the writing guidelines provided in this Teacher's Guide on pages 78 and 79 at the back of this book, in addition to the Practice Book.

The *Happy Handwriting* course prioritises the introduction of the correct movements to form lower-case letters (letter formation), followed by their capital formations. The letters are introduced in order of letter movement families, based on the formation of the letters. If a child is struggling with consistently writing one family of letters, additional practice material is provided.

The letter formation families

The four families are:

- The Curly Caterpillar family: anti-clockwise round, exemplified by the letter c
  - c a d g o q and e s f
- The Long Ladder family: down and off in another direction, exemplified by the letter l
  - i l t and u y j k
- The Robot family: down and retrace upwards, exemplified by the letter r
  - r n m and h b p
- The Zigzag family: straight, sharp turn, exemplified by the letter z
  - v w x z

Letter formation for left-handers

The formation of some letters is slightly different for some left-handed children, who 'pull' the lines right to left, whereas right-handers will 'push' lines left to right. These letters are lower-case t and f and capitals A, E, F, H, J and T.

Joining letters in Key Stage 2

In Key Stage 1, *Happy Handwriting* teaches five main joins between letters:

1. Diagonal joins to letters without ascenders (for example: *ai*)
2. Diagonal joins to letters with ascenders (for example: *ch*)
3. Horizontal joins to letters without ascenders (for example: *wa*)
4. Horizontal joins to letters with ascenders (for example: *wh*)
5. Joins to round (anti-clockwise) letters (for example: *ad*).

Although Years 4 and 5 are when most children learn to produce joins efficiently, some children in Years 5 and 6 may still be establishing these joins as automatic movements. In Years 5 and 6, *Happy Handwriting* also offers additional practice of the tricky or less frequent joins. All Key Stage 2 writers also need to know which letters not to join for maximum efficiency, and to focus on the size and spacing of letters and joins.

Break letters

Happy Handwriting uses a lower-case script where most letters have an exit stroke or 'flick', then moves into a mostly joined script where joins are natural and promote fluency and flow in writing. In *Happy Handwriting*, these letters do not join to letters following them: b, g, j, p, q, x, y, z, s. Most adults use an efficient semi-joined script when they write, and *Happy Handwriting* prepares children to learn this as early as possible.

Learning the alphabet

Knowing the names of the letters helps with phonics and spelling. Call a letter by its name, rather than the sound associated with it. If children learn the letter name when they learn the movement for the lower-case letter, they can then learn the capital letter which has the same name. Alphabetical order of letter names is an easily learned sequence that lasts a lifetime. It enables children to use dictionaries and alphabetical order – and it is one system that is not changing in this digital age! *Happy Handwriting* encourages you to sing the classic alphabet song – even in Key Stage 2 – to ensure everyone is secure in their alphabet knowledge, and to do the additional alphabet activities on page 77 of this guide. There are even more alphabet activities available in the *Happy Handwriting* printable resources.

Writing a school handwriting policy

A handwriting policy for your school needs to include handwriting in all its forms – using pens, pencils and digital tools – and for all its purposes, from note-taking to special presentation. Today, we recognise that children need to develop legibility, fluency and speed in their handwriting and that neatness is not the only criterion for good handwriting. There is a trade-off between efficiency and neatness, and children will need to learn to consciously adjust the balance between these two important aspects of handwriting. The simple, efficient font used by *Happy Handwriting* makes this easier for children to achieve.

The process of developing a handwriting policy gives teachers the chance to discuss the criteria for a successful handwriting curriculum. To develop a handwriting policy, you will need to include all classroom staff in the discussion of: the goals of the school handwriting curriculum, the way the curriculum is to be taught, and how the impact of the teaching is to be assessed. These criteria are summarised as the intent, implementation and impact of the handwriting curriculum (Ofsted, 2019). To ensure you have addressed these issues in your policy, you can discuss the answers to these questions:

- Is your handwriting curriculum based on evidence-based practice?
- Is the handwriting curriculum both ambitious and designed to give all children the skills needed to communicate by hand?
- Is the curriculum coherently planned and sequenced for the cumulative acquisition of knowledge and skills?
- Do teachers have training and support to enable them to teach handwriting effectively?
- Do teachers have a good knowledge of the development of handwriting skills?
- Do teachers create an environment that optimises learning conditions?
- Do the resources and materials support a coherently planned curriculum?
- Do teachers present the subject matter clearly?
- Do teachers check children's understanding systematically, identify misconceptions accurately and provide clear, direct feedback?
- Do teachers and leaders use assessment well – for example, to check understanding and inform teaching?

Happy Handwriting can be used to meet all these criteria, because it is systematically and cumulatively planned on the basis of research and evidence, and provides a full range of resources. *Happy Handwriting* sets ambitious goals for children's learning and provides additional materials for children who need them.

To develop a school policy, we recommend you should meet to discuss these aspects of this *Happy Handwriting* Teacher's Guide:

- the Collins Handwriting font – its features and where you can use it in school materials
- the order of introduction of letter movements and joins
- lesson processes and use of the *Happy Handwriting* resources in class
- assessment and recording
- using the *Happy Handwriting* additional materials to promote progress
- additional practice and parent/carer involvement activities.

An example of a school handwriting policy is included in the printable materials for discussion.

A handwriting policy should include, but not be limited to, the following content, which is discussed in this Teacher's Guide:

- the handwriting scheme used in school (including letter formations and joins)
- handwriting in the curriculum (what standards of presentation you have agreed)
- language about handwriting to promote clarity
- key issues in teaching handwriting
- resources used in school
- school approaches to teaching handwriting
- organisation of handwriting
- support for left-handed writers
- assessment of handwriting
- support for struggling writers
- involving parents and carers with handwriting.

The printable materials that are part of *Happy Handwriting* include:

- a chart of statutory assessment goals for handwriting and the goals of *Happy Handwriting*
- an example of a handwriting policy to discuss
- a glossary of terms about handwriting for each Key Stage so that both staff and children use a shared vocabulary and establish complete clarity about handwriting
- additional assessment and support materials.

You may want to develop a handwriting and presentation policy, commenting on presentation across the curriculum, or you may feel it is more useful to include presentation (and handwriting) in subject policies.

Glossary of terms (Key Stage 2)

- **Ascender**: the part of the letter that goes above the main body (t is shorter than others)
- **Baseline**: the line that the body of a short letter sits on
- **Bottom line**: the line in writing guidelines that descenders go down to
- **Break letter**: a letter that does not join to letters following it: *b, g, j, p, q, x, y, z, s*
- **Capital letter**: the term used in *Happy Handwriting* for upper-case letters
- **Cross bar**: the stroke going across *t, f* and some capitals
- **Descender**: the part of the letter that goes below the baseline
- **Diagonal join:** a join from the bottom of a letter
- **Exit stroke or flick**: letters that finish on the baseline may have a final flick in the forwards direction, which can become a join
- **Horizontal join**: a join from the top of a letter
- **Join**: the writing movement between one letter and the next; *Happy Handwriting* uses five main joins
- **Lower-case letter**: the term used in *Happy Handwriting* for a small letter
- **Round letter**: the round part of the letter body, where there is an anti-clockwise curve
- **Short letter** (or x-height letter): a letter without an ascender or descender that is the same height as an *x*
- **Starting dot**: the point at which the letter should be started in order to facilitate good movement
- **Tall letter**: a letter with an ascender that goes to the top line of the guidelines

Handwriting in the National Curriculum for Upper Key Stage 2

The National Curriculum for English programmes of study for writing at Key Stage 2 includes:

- transcription (spelling and handwriting)
- composition (articulating ideas and structuring them in speech and writing).

The programmes of study specify that, by the end of Year 6, children's reading and writing should be sufficiently fluent and effortless for them to manage the general demands of the curriculum. This includes automatic, effortless handwriting.

Statutory requirements (Upper Key Stage 2)

Pupils should be taught to 'write legibly, fluently and with increasing speed by choosing which shape of a letter to use when given choices and deciding whether or not to join specific letters; choosing the writing implement that is best suited for a task.'

Notes and guidance (non-statutory)

In Upper Key Stage 2, 'pupils should continue to practise handwriting and be encouraged to increase the speed of it, so that problems with forming letters do not get in the way of their writing down what they want to say. They should be clear about what standard of handwriting is appropriate for a particular task, for example, quick notes or a final handwritten version. They should also be taught to use an unjoined style, for example, for labelling a diagram or data, writing an email address, or for algebra and capital letters, for example, for filling in a form.'

Teaching priorities for Happy Handwriting in Year 5 (and 6)

If children can learn fluent handwriting, it will help them to write across the curriculum. Year 5 priorities are:

- joining correctly where appropriate (and knowing where not to)
- consolidating difficult joins (revising regularly)
- using appropriate spacing between letters and punctuation marks
- increasing speed
- choosing when to focus on speed, while retaining legibility
- placing and spacing punctuation correctly
- printing and using block capital letters when appropriate
- self-evaluating the formation, orientation, legibility, and speed of their writing, according to task
- using first and second letter alphabetical order.

In Year 5, all children should be able to:

- produce letter movements automatically
- make most joins automatically
- write ascenders and descenders consistently
- produce common letter combinations automatically.

This Year 5 Teacher's Guide contains advice and activities to diagnose the needs of children who may need more letter formation work to increase speed and automaticity. Additional activities for letter formation practice are available in this guide, pages 74–76, and in the printable resources.

The teaching focus for each week (Year 5)

Term 1	Handwriting focus
1	Writing quickly and neatly
2	Joining to and from *e*
3	Joining to and from *r*
4	Revising key joins: diagonal joins
5	Ascenders and descenders
6	Placing and spacing punctuation in sentences
7	Writing quickly
8	Writing neatly
9	Alphabetical order
10	Self-assessment
Term 2	
11	Joining to and from *t*
12	Joining to and from *f*
13	Revising key joins: horizontal joins
14	Revising break letters: *y, j, g, p*
15	Getting the height right: capital letters
16	Placing and spacing punctuation: commas and bullet points
17	Writing direct speech
18	Placing and spacing: apostrophes
19	Alphabetical order: to the second letter
20	Self-assessment
Term 3	
21	Writing notes quickly
22	Joining to and from *k*
23	Revising key joins: joins to round letters
24	Getting the height right
25	Printing and labelling
26	Placing and spacing punctuation: speech marks
27	Writing quickly: words per minute
28	Writing neatly: a formal letter
29	Spacing items in a list
30	Self-assessment

Name/Group: _____ Date: _____

Letter formations

a b c d e f g
h i j k l m n
o p q r s t u
v w x y z

A B C D E F
G H I J K L M
N O P Q R S T
U V W X Y Z

Teaching handwriting in Year 5

Writing position

Good writing position allows writers to use their core and shoulder muscles for support and to move their arms. The child's chair should be at a comfortable height so that they can place both feet flat on the floor for stability. Young writers need space to accommodate wide elbow positioning.

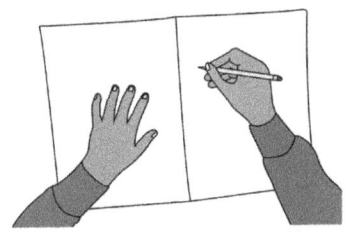

Right-handed children should place the paper or book slightly to the right and slant the paper slightly to the left. Right-handed children should steady the paper or book with their left hand.

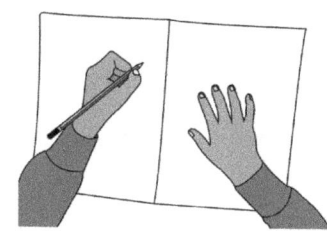

Left-handed children should place the paper or book slightly to the left and slant the paper slightly to the right. Left-handed children should steady the paper or book with their right hand.

Pencil (or pen) grip

To develop a fluent and fast handwriting style, children must develop a controlled pencil/pen grip that is comfortable for them. There are a number of perfectly acceptable ways to hold a pencil or pen, but many children hold the writing implement between the thumb and index finger with the pencil/pen supported on the middle finger and the ring and little fingers gently curled inwards. This gives an open, wide space, which means that the movement comes from the fingers and produces a flexible hold that does not exhaust the writer.

Any grip with a number of points of contact, and also some flexibility, is suitable if it is comfortable. Too tight a grip prevents free-flowing handwriting and is exhausting for the child. If children grip the pencil too tightly, they become tense in the arm and shoulder and place too much pressure on the paper, so this is something to watch for.

Hand preference

Around 10% of any population will prefer to write with their left hand. There are simple ways to support the details of posture, paper positioning, pencil grip and so on that can make handwriting comfortable for all children, left- or right-handed.

Left-handed children

- Remember to model letter formation and joining specifically for left-handed children, with your left hand. You may also need to remind children which hand they write with.
- Left-handed children may benefit from sitting to the left of right-handed children to avoid elbow clashes.
- Left-handers may write better if they sit on a slightly higher chair so that they are further 'above' the writing.

- Left-handed children should tilt the paper to the right and steady the paper with a right hand. This takes practice.
- Left-handed children may benefit from holding the pencil/pen about 1.5 cm higher up the shaft than right-handed children. This helps prevent smudging, but is harder to control.
- Left-handed children may find that fountain pens dig into the paper, but can still enjoy using them.

Writing from left to right is more difficult for left-handed children because of the nature of our writing system. They may need more attention in the classroom to ensure that they do not learn bad habits of position, posture and pen hold, which will prevent the development of fast, fluent and legible writing.

Choice of medium

Pencils are an ideal medium to start handwriting, but in Key Stage 2 a fibre-tipped pen that provides a good degree of friction gives young writers control over their writing. Some types of 'slippery' ink in ball-point pens can make good letter formation and joining even more difficult, so avoid these types of ink. In Year 5, writers may want to experiment with fountain pens and shaped nibs. These are not necessarily the most efficient implements, and might be best used only on certain tasks, but they can add personal style and some fun to handwriting!

Teaching the Happy Handwriting lessons

Handwriting teaching routines

We recommend teaching two focused handwriting lessons per week for all children in Year 5, using the slideshow presentation and Practice Book. Each unit has a handwriting and spelling focus built in. There is a range of additional activities that children in Year 5 can do.

For children who will benefit from more practice, the two main handwriting lessons can be supplemented with additional short practice sessions, to establish a join or letter movement. At Year 5, the *Happy Handwriting* course provides the following resources for each teaching week:

Happy Handwriting resource	Lesson goal	Location	Suggested for
Presentations	Introduction of joins and movements	Available to download	All children
Practice Book (Lesson 1)	Introducing and practising the new material using the Practice Book	Practice Book and exercise book	All children
Practice Book (Lesson 2)	Practising the unit focus using the additional resources	Practice Book and exercise book	All children
Home Practice sheets	Practising spelling and handwriting	Available to download	All children
Further practice	Practising the unit focus	Suggested activity in the lesson plan	Groups of children who may need to practise
Additional Practice sheets	Practising the unit focus using the sheet	Copiable sheets in this Teacher's Guide	Children struggling with this point
Extra Practice sheets	Practising the basic letter forms or joins to build fluency	Copiable sheets in this Teacher's Guide	Children struggling with fluency and automaticity, following diagnostic assessment
Printable Practice sheets	Revising and revisiting important basics	Copiable sheets in the printable resources for the year	Children struggling with fluency and automaticity, following diagnostic assessment

Start each lesson with a 'settling routine', including a short stretching routine to get the children's muscles ready to write. If any children do not know the alphabet, you may also want to sing the alphabet song, as it is an easy way to learn. Ensure that the children are seated in the correct writing position at a table with their feet on the floor and their book or paper arranged so that they can write, and that they are gripping their pencils/pens appropriately.

The 'settling routine':

- stretch the arms above the head
- stretch arms out in front and wiggle fingers
- hunch and drop shoulders and push spine backwards
- rotate wrists and rotate ankles
- wriggle and stretch fingers
- ready to write!

During handwriting teaching, it is vital to observe the children doing the writing in the Practice Book so that you can check they are making the correct letter and join movements. These movements should be continuous, and children should not take the pencil/pen off the paper between letters. Dotting i or j or crossing t should be done when the word or letter sequence is finished.

Involving parents and carers in handwriting improvement

Handwriting benefits from regular, frequent practice, and most parents and carers are happy to support their children to do a short handwriting activity. A small, regular additional practice session can make a great deal of difference and does not provide too much challenge for most children. *Happy Handwriting* includes printable sheets suitable for children to complete at home, where any degree of encouragement from carers or other family members is helpful. Each sheet has a handwriting and spelling learning point, because spelling and handwriting practice can be usefully combined. In Key Stage 2, some home practice sheets require additional space for writing. We recommend you supply each child with a print out of the four-line writing guidelines (pages 78–79) to ensure they have access to the appropriate writing resources. The emphasis of home practice should be short bursts of practice, with plenty of praise, rather than completing the whole sheet.

Look Cover Write Check (LCWC)

Home handwriting sheets also have a spelling element, because learning spelling and handwriting are complementary activities. When asking children in Year 5 to learn the spelling of words, we recommend using the Look Cover Write Check strategy. This involves:

- looking very carefully at the words and saying the name of each letter aloud (then shutting your eyes and 'seeing' the letters on your eyelids)
- covering up the word
- writing the word without looking back at it
- checking to see if it is correct.

The child can do this as many times as necessary. A folded 'fan' of paper (or book page) can give multiple opportunities.

Unit 1: Writing quickly and neatly

	Lesson 1	**Lesson 2**	**Practice**
	Class or group seated at tables	*Class or group seated at tables*	*Class or group seated at tables*
Objective	To discuss writing quickly.	To discuss writing neatly.	To consolidate writing quickly and neatly.
Resources	– Practice Book Page 3, Part 1 – Presentation Unit 1, Part 1 – Pencil or pen	– Practice Book Page 3, Part 2 – Presentation Unit 1, Part 2 – Pencil or pen	– Additional Practice sheet 1 – Presentation Unit 1, Part 3 – Pencil or pen
Teaching	• **Settling routine and hand warm-up** • Tell children that, this year, they will learn to make choices about whether neatness or speed is most important. • **Practice Book:** Ask children to copy the words quickly. • Use the **Presentation** to show the sentences, or ask children to look in their **Practice Book**. Ask children to copy the sentences into their books as quickly as they can.	• **Settling routine** • **Practice Book:** Ask children to copy the sentence. • Use the **Presentation** to show the shopping list, or ask children to look in their **Practice Book**. Ask children to copy the list into their books as neatly as they can.	• **Settling routine** • **Additional Practice sheet:** Ask children to copy the sentence neatly. • **Additional Practice sheet:** Ask children to copy the words quickly. • **Additional Practice sheet:** Use the **Presentation** to show the passage. Ask children to copy out the passage in their neatest handwriting into their books.
Assessment criterion	Can the child: – write quickly and analyse next steps?	– write neatly and analyse next steps?	– write quickly and neatly?
Further practice	To further practise writing quickly and neatly, you could ask children to: 1. write their name 10 times as quickly as possible 2. write an invitation to a party, using their neatest handwriting.		

Unit 2: Joining to and from *e*

	Lesson 1	Lesson 2	Practice
	Whole class seated at tables	*Class or groups seated at tables*	*Whole class or groups seated at tables*
Objective	To consolidate joins to and from *e*.	To practise joining *e*.	To practise joining *e*.
Resources	– Practice Book Page 4, Part 1 – Presentation Unit 2, Part 1 – Pencil or pen	– Practice Book Page 4, Part 2 – Presentation Unit 2, Part 2 – Pencil or pen	– Additional Practice sheet 2 – Presentation Unit 2, Part 3 – Pencil or pen
Teaching	• **Settling routine and hand warm-up** • Tell children that *e* begins in an unusual place and that joining from it is difficult. • Use the **Presentation** to introduce the joins: *re, ee, el*. • **Practice Book:** Ask children to copy the letters and words. Use the **Presentation** to show the news article, or ask children to look in their **Practice Book:** Ask children to copy the passage into their books.	• **Settling routine** • **Practice Book:** Ask children to copy the words. Use the **Presentation** to show the rest of the news article, or ask children to look in their **Practice Book:** Ask children to copy the passage into their books, paying attention to the joins that they found difficult in the previous lesson.	• **Settling routine** • **Additional Practice sheet:** Ask children to copy the joins quickly: *de, fe, en, ce*. • **Additional Practice sheet:** Ask children to fill in the missing words and copy the sentence neatly.
Assessment criterion	**Can the child:** – *join to and from e with the joins at an appropriate height?*	– *join to and from e with the joins at an appropriate height, being careful not to join to break letters?*	– *join to and from e with the joins at an appropriate height, being careful not to join to break letters?*
Further practice	To further practise joining to and from *e*, you could ask children to: 1. write out these target words on plain paper/cards, making sure the joins are correct: *free, letter, elf, defence, repeat, sure* 2. write one sentence that includes the word *'centre'*, and one sentence that includes a word ending with *-er* (for example: *louder, hamster, ladder, winter*).		

Lesson plan

Unit 3: Joining to and from *r*

	Lesson 1	Lesson 2	Practice
	Whole class seated at tables	*Class or groups seated at tables*	*Whole class or groups seated at tables*
Objective	To consolidate joins to and from *r*.	To practise joining *r*.	To practise joining *r*.
Resources	– Practice Book Page 5, Part 1 – Presentation Unit 3, Part 1 – Pencil or pen	– Practice Book Page 5, Part 2 – Presentation Unit 3, Part 2 – Pencil or pen	– Additional Practice sheet 3 – Presentation Unit 3, Part 3 – Pencil or pen
Teaching	• Settling routine and hand warm-up • Tell children that joining to *r* is less complicated than joining from it. • Use the **Presentation** to introduce the joins: *or, ere, are, rl*. • **Practice Book:** Ask children to copy the joins. • Use the **Presentation** to show the passage, or ask children to look in their **Practice Book**. Ask children to copy the passage into their books.	• Settling routine • **Practice Book:** Ask children to copy the words. • **Practice Book:** Ask children to use the words to complete the passage. Ask children to copy the completed passage into their books. You can display the passage using the **Presentation** if necessary.	• Settling routine • **Additional Practice sheet:** Ask children to copy the sentence. • **Additional Practice sheet:** Ask children to copy the words quickly. • **Additional Practice sheet:** Ask children to copy the words neatly.
Assessment criterion	Can the child: – join to and from *r* with the joins at an appropriate height?	– join to and from *r* with the joins at an appropriate height?	– join to and from *r* with the joins at an appropriate height?
Further practice	To further practise joining to and from r, you could ask children to: 1. write out these target words on plain paper/cards, making sure the joins are correct: *heard, herd, alter, ride, alter* 2. pick two words with a tricky join from *r* and write two sentences including these words.		

Happy Handwriting

Lesson plan

Unit 4: Revising key joins: diagonal joins

	Lesson 1	Lesson 2	Practice
	Whole class seated at tables	*Class or groups seated at tables*	*Whole class or groups seated at tables*
Objective	To revise diagonal joins.	To practise diagonal joins.	To consolidate diagonal joins.
Resources	– Practice Book Page 6, Part 1 – Presentation Unit 4, Part 1 – Pencil or pen	– Practice Book: Page 6, Part 2 – Presentation Unit 4, Part 2 – Pencil or pen	– Additional Practice sheet 4 – Presentation Unit 4, Part 3 – Pencil or pen
Teaching	• Settling routine and hand warm-up • Remind children that the letter *t* is slightly shorter than other letters with ascenders. • Use the **Presentation** to introduce the joins: *ant, ent, al, er*. • Use the **Presentation** to show the beginning of the letter, or ask children to look in their **Practice Book**. Ask children to copy it into their books.	• Settling routine • **Practice Book:** Ask children to add the suffix *-ant* or *-ent*, then copy out the new word. • Use the **Presentation** to show the rest of the letter, or ask children to look in their **Practice Book**. Ask children to copy it into their books.	• Settling routine • **Additional Practice sheet:** Ask children to copy the sentence. • **Additional Practice sheet:** Ask children to copy the words. • **Additional Practice sheet:** Use the **Presentation** to show the question. Ask children to copy it into their books, then answer it.
Assessment criterion	Can the child: – join diagonally?	– join diagonally?	– join diagonally?
Further practice	To further practise diagonal joins, you could ask children to: 1. write comparative sentences using *tall/taller/tallest*, *small/smaller/smallest* and *big/bigger/biggest* 2. speed-write *-ent* and *-ant* words in a race against other players.		

Unit 5: Ascenders and descenders

	Lesson 1	Lesson 2	Practice
	Whole class seated at tables	*Class or groups seated at tables*	*Whole class or groups seated at tables*
Objective	To practise ascenders and descenders.	To practise ascenders and descenders.	To consolidate ascenders and descenders.
Resources	– Practice Book Page 7, Part 1 – Presentation Unit 5, Part 1 – Pencil or pen	– Practice Book Page 7, Part 2 – Presentation Unit 5, Part 2 – Pencil or pen	– Additional Practice sheet 5 – Presentation Unit 5, Part 3 – Pencil or pen
Teaching	• Settling routine and hand warm-up • Remind children that *g* doesn't join and that *t* is shorter than *h*. • Use the **Presentation** to show the relative sizes of letters. • **Practice Book:** Ask children to copy the words. • Use the **Presentation** to show the fact, or ask children to look in their **Practice Book**. Ask children to copy the fact into their books, making sure that the capital and tall letters are the correct heights.	• Settling routine • **Practice Book:** Ask children to copy the words. • **Practice Book:** Ask children to add the suffix -*y* (-*ibly*), then copy out the new word. • Use the **Presentation** to show the fact or ask children to look in their **Practice Book**. Ask children to copy the fact into their books, making sure that the capital and tall letters are the correct heights.	• Settling routine • **Additional Practice sheet:** Ask children to copy the sentence. • **Additional Practice sheet:** Ask children to copy the sentences, making sure that the capital letters and tall letters are the correct heights.
Assessment criterion	Can the child: – use ascenders and descenders accurately?	– use ascenders and descenders accurately?	– use ascenders and descenders accurately?
Further practice	To further practise ascenders and descenders, you could ask children to: 1. group letters of the alphabet into ascenders, descenders and other types of letter 2. make up a rhyming poem using the words *rough*, *enough* and *tough*.		

Lesson plan

Unit 6: Placing and spacing punctuation in sentences

	Lesson 1	Lesson 2	Practice
	Whole class seated at tables	*Class or groups seated at tables*	*Whole class or groups seated at tables*
Objective	To place and space punctuation.	To practise placing and spacing punctuation.	To consolidate placing and spacing punctuation.
Resources	– Practice Book Page 8, Part 1 – Presentation Unit 6, Part 1 – Pencil or pen	– Practice Book Page 8, Part 2 – Presentation Unit 6, Part 2 – Pencil or pen	– Additional Practice sheet 6 – Presentation Unit 6, Part 3 – Pencil or pen
Teaching	• Settling routine and hand warm-up • Tell children that using capital letters and punctuation changes the spaces between words. • Use the **Presentation** to discuss the capitalisation of nouns. • **Practice Book:** Ask children to copy the words. • Use the **Presentation** to show the passage, or ask children to look in their **Practice Book**: Ask children to correct the capital letters and full stops, then copy the passage into their books. Show the corrected version in the **Presentation** and point out how the capital letters and full stops have changed the spacings.	• Settling routine • **Practice Book:** Ask children to copy the words. • Use the **Presentation** to show the sentences, or ask children to look in their **Practice Book**. Ask children to correct the capital letters and question marks, then copy the questions into their books. Show the corrected version in the **Presentation** and point out how the capital letters and question marks have changed the spacings.	• Settling routine • **Additional Practice sheet:** Ask children to copy the sentence. • **Additional Practice sheet:** Ask children to copy the exclamations into their books. • Use the **Presentation** to show the passage, or ask children to look at their **Additional Practice sheet**: Ask children to correct the capital letters and punctuation, then copy the sentences into their books. Show the corrected version in the **Presentation** and point out how the capital letters and punctuation have changed the spacings.
Assessment criterion	Can the child: – recognise the difference between spacing when adding capital letters and full stops?	– place and space capital letters and question marks correctly?	– place and space capital letters, question marks and exclamation marks correctly?
Further practice	To further practise placing and spacing punctuation, you could ask children to: 1. write a sentence or two with no full stops or question marks, then swap with a partner and correct each other's sentences 2. write the first line of their address, or their full name, using correct spacing for the capital letters.		

22   Happy Handwriting

Unit 7: Writing quickly

	Lesson 1	Lesson 2	Practice
	Whole class seated at tables	*Class or groups seated at tables*	*Whole class or groups seated at tables*
Objective	To write quickly.	To write quickly.	To write quickly.
Resources	– Practice Book Page 9, Part 1 – Presentation Unit 7, Part 1 – Pencil or pen	– Practice Book Page 9, Part 2 – Presentation Unit 7, Part 2 – Pencil or pen	– Additional Practice sheet 7 – Presentation Unit 7, Part 3 – Pencil or pen
Teaching	• Settling routine and hand warm-up • Emphasise the need to make fast writing legible, not rushed. • Use the **Presentation** to show the passage, or ask children to look in their **Practice Book**. Ask children to copy the passage quickly into their books and time themselves. How long did it take them to write 37 readable words?	• Settling routine • Use the **Presentation** to show the passage, or ask children to look in their **Practice Book**. Ask children to copy the passage quickly into their books and time themselves. How long did it take them to write 38 readable words?	• Settling routine • **Additional Practice sheet:** Ask children to copy the sentence quickly. • **Additional Practice sheet:** Ask children to write the notes as full sentences.
Assessment criterion	Can the child: – write quickly and legibly, and time their writing?	– write quickly and neatly, and time their writing?	– write quickly and neatly?
Further practice	To further practise writing quickly, you could ask children to: 1. write out the lyrics to a song as quickly as they can 2. write out a joke quickly and then ask a friend if they are able to read it.		

Unit 8: Writing neatly

	Lesson 1	Lesson 2	Practice
	Whole class seated at tables	*Class or groups seated at tables*	*Whole class or groups seated at tables*
Objective	To write neatly.	To write neatly.	To write neatly.
Resources	– Practice Book Page 10, Part 1 – Presentation Unit 8, Part 1 – Pencil or pen	– Practice Book Page 10, Part 2 – Presentation Unit 8, Part 2 – Pencil or pen	– Additional Practice sheet 8 – Presentation Unit 8, Part 3 – Pencil or pen
Teaching	• **Settling routine and hand warm-up** • Tell children to use neat handwriting when they think the reader will appreciate it. • **Practice Book:** Ask children to copy the words neatly. • Use the **Presentation** to show the passage, or ask children to look in their **Practice Book**. Ask children to copy the passage into their books, using their best handwriting.	• **Settling routine** • Use the **Presentation** to show the words, or ask children to look in their **Practice Book**. Ask children to use the words to write a 'thank you' message in their books, using their best handwriting.	• **Settling routine** • **Additional Practice sheet:** Ask children to copy the sentence neatly. • **Additional Practice sheet:** Look at the passage (and see the **Presentation**). Ask children to correct the capital letters and punctuation, then copy the passage into their books in their best handwriting. Show the corrected version in the **Presentation**.
Assessment criterion	Can the child: – write neatly?	– write neatly?	– write neatly?
Further practice	To further practise writing neatly, you could ask children to: 1. write a note to a teacher or teaching assistant to thank them for their support 2. write one of the practice sentences from this unit three times, then analyse which attempt is best and why.		

Lesson plan

Unit 9: Alphabetical order

	Lesson 1	Lesson 2	Practice
	Whole class seated at tables	*Class or groups seated at tables*	*Whole class or groups seated at tables*
Objective	To put words in alphabetical order using the first letter.	To put words in alphabetical order using the second letter.	To put words in alphabetical order using the first and second letters.
Resources	– Practice Book Page 11, Part 1 – Presentation Unit 9, Part 1 – Pencil or pen	– Practice Book Page 11, Part 2 – Presentation Unit 9, Part 2 – Pencil or pen	– Additional Practice sheet 9 – Presentation Unit 9, Part 3 – Pencil or pen
Teaching	• Settling routine and hand warm-up • **Practice Book:** Ask children to copy the words. • **Practice Book:** Ask children to write the list in alphabetical order.	• Settling routine • **Practice Book:** Ask children to copy the sentences. • **Practice Book:** Ask children to write the list of names in alphabetical order, using the second letter of each name.	• Settling routine • **Additional Practice sheet:** Ask children to copy the sentence neatly. • **Additional Practice sheet:** Ask children to write the list in alphabetical order. Remind children that if words start with the same first letter, they need to look at the second letter.
Assessment criterion	Can the child: – put words in alphabetical order using the first letter?	– put words in alphabetical order using the second letter?	– put words in alphabetical order using the first and second letter?
Further practice	To further practise alphabetical order, you could ask children to: 1. write out the alphabet so they can use it for reference 2. put the names of some their classmates in alphabetical order.		

Happy Handwriting

Unit 10: Self-assessment

	Lesson 1	Lesson 2	Lesson 3
	Whole class seated at tables	*Class or groups seated at tables*	*Class or groups seated at tables*
Objective	To self-assess handwriting.	To self-assess handwriting.	To self-assess handwriting.
Resources	– Practice Book Page 12, Part 1 – Presentation Unit 10, Part 1 – Pencil or pen	– Practice Book Page 12, Part 2 – Presentation Unit 10, Part 2 – Pencil or pen	– Paper or exercise book – Pencil or pen
Teaching	• Settling routine and hand warm-up • Have a discussion in class to remind children of the criteria for good handwriting (see page 20). • Use the **Presentation** to show the sentence. Ask children to correct the capital letters and full stops, then copy the sentence neatly. Show the corrected version in the **Presentation**. • Use the **Presentation** to show the passage, or ask children to look in their **Practice Book**. Ask children to correct the capital letters and punctuation, then copy the passage quickly. They should time themselves to see how long it takes. Show the corrected version in the **Presentation**. • Use the **Presentation** to model how to assess their writing.	• Settling routine • Use the **Presentation** to show the sentence. Ask children to correct the capital letters and full stops, then copy the sentence quickly. Show the corrected version in the **Presentation**. • Use the **Presentation** to show the passage, or ask children to look in their **Practice Book**. Ask children to correct the capital letters and punctuation, then copy the passage quickly. They should time themselves to see how long it takes. Show the corrected version in the **Presentation**. • Use the **Presentation** to model how to assess their writing.	• Settling routine • Children look through their independent writing and self-assess by completing the following sentences: This term I have improved _____. I need to practise _____.
Assessment criterion	Can the child: – assess their own handwriting?	– assess their own handwriting?	– complete the following sentences? This term I have improved _____. I need to practise _____.
Further practice	To further practise their handwriting, you could ask children to: 1. write a neat paragraph about their favourite things to do at the weekend 2. write some quick notes about what they saw on the way to school that morning.		

Unit 11: Joining to and from *t*

	Lesson 1	Lesson 2	Practice
	Whole class seated at tables	*Class or groups seated at tables*	*Whole class or groups seated at tables*
Objective	To consolidate joins to and from *t*.	To practise joining *t*.	To practise joining *t*.
Resources	– Practice Book Page 13, Part 1 – Presentation Unit 11, Part 1 – Pencil or pen	– Practice Book Page 13, Part 2 – Presentation Unit 11, Part 2 – Pencil or pen	– Additional Practice sheet 11 – Presentation Unit 11, Part 3 – Pencil or pen
Teaching	• Settling routine and hand warm-up • Remind children to check that their *t* is the right height and that the joins are diagonal. • **Practice Book:** Ask children to copy the sentence. • Use the **Presentation** to show the joins in the words. • **Practice Book:** Ask children to copy the words. • Use the **Presentation** to show the sentences.	• Settling routine • **Practice Book:** Ask children to copy the words. • **Practice Book:** Ask children to use the words to complete the sentences. Ask children to copy the completed sentences. You can display them in the **Presentation** if necessary.	• Settling routine • **Additional Practice sheet:** Ask children to copy the sentence. • **Additional Practice sheet:** Ask children to copy the sentence neatly.
Assessment criterion	Can the child: – join to and from *t* diagonally?	– join to and from *t* diagonally?	– join to and from *t* diagonally?
Further practice	To further practise joining to and from *t*, you could ask children to: 1. write out these target words on plain paper/cards, making sure that the joins are correct: *interact, interrupt, interesting* 2. pick two words that they have written in this unit, and write two sentences including these words.		

Happy Handwriting

Unit 12: Joining to and from *f*

	Lesson 1	Lesson 2	Practice
	Whole class seated at tables	*Class or groups seated at tables*	*Whole class or groups seated at tables*
Objective	To consolidate joins to and from *f*.	To practise joining *f*.	To practise joining *f*.
Resources	– Practice Book Page 14, Part 1 – Presentation Unit 12, Part 1 – Pencil or pen	– Practice Book Page 14, Part 2 – Presentation Unit 12, Part 2 – Pencil or pen	– Additional Practice sheet 12 – Presentation Unit 12, Part 3 – Pencil or pen
Teaching	• Settling routine and hand warm-up • Tell children that letters join to *f* with a diagonal join but join from *f* using a horizontal join. • **Practice Book:** Ask children to copy the sentence. • Use the **Presentation** to show the joins in the words. • **Practice Book:** Ask children to copy the words. • **Practice Book:** Ask children to copy the sentence.	• Settling routine • **Practice Book:** Ask children to copy the sentence: *Be careful how you write f.* • **Practice Book:** Ask children to copy the sentences quickly.	• Settling routine • **Additional Practice sheet:** Ask children to copy the sentence. • **Additional Practice sheet:** Ask children to complete the table.
Assessment criterion	Can the child: – join to and from *f*?	– join to and from *f*?	– join to and from *f*?
Further practice	To further practise joining to and from *f*, you could ask children to: 1. turn these adjectives into adverbs (ending in *-fully*), making sure the joins are correct: *careful, helpful, dreadful, useful, playful* 2. pick two words that they have written in this unit, and write two sentences including these words.		

Lesson plan

Unit 13: Revising key joins: horizontal joins

	Lesson 1	Lesson 2	Practice
	Whole class seated at tables	*Class or groups seated at tables*	*Whole class or groups seated at tables*
Objective	To revise horizontal joins.	To practise horizontal joins.	To consolidate horizontal joins.
Resources	– Practice Book Page 15, Part 1 – Presentation Unit 13, Part 1 – Pencil or pen	– Practice Book Page 15, Part 2 – Presentation Unit 13, Part 2 – Pencil or pen	– Additional Practice sheet 13 – Presentation Unit 13, Part 3 – Pencil or pen
Teaching	• Settling routine and hand warm-up • Tell children that horizontal joins can go along to short letters or up to tall letters. • Use the **Presentation** to show the joins in the words. • **Practice Book:** Ask children to copy the words. • **Practice Book:** Ask children to copy the sentences.	• Settling routine • **Practice Book:** Ask children to copy the sentence. • **Practice Book:** Ask children to complete the table with past-tense verbs:	• Settling routine • **Additional Practice sheet:** Ask children to copy the words quickly. • **Additional Practice sheet:** Ask children to copy the poem neatly into their books.
Assessment criterion	Can the child: – join from *o*, *w* and *v*?	– join from *o*, *w* and *v*?	– join from *o*, *w* and *v*?
Further practice	To further practise horizontal joins, you could ask children to: 1. write another poem using the words *live*, *love*, *walk* and *brave* 2. turn these words into adverbs by adding -*ly*: *live*, *love*, *brave*.		

Happy Handwriting

Lesson plan

Unit 14: Revising break letters: y, j, g, p

	Lesson 1	Lesson 2	Practice
	Whole class seated at tables	*Class or groups seated at tables*	*Whole class or groups seated at tables*
Objective	To revise break letters.	To practise break letters.	To consolidate break letters.
Resources	– Practice Book Page 16, Part 1 – Presentation Unit 14, Part 1 – Pencil or pen	– Practice Book Page 16, Part 2 – Presentation Unit 14, Part 2 – Pencil or pen	– Additional Practice sheet 14 – Presentation Unit 14, Part 3 – Pencil or pen
Teaching	• Settling routine and hand warm-up • Remind children to pay careful attention to the length of their descenders. Explain that y, j, g, p do not join to the next letter. • **Practice Book:** Ask children to copy the sentence. • Use the **Presentation** to demonstrate that some of the letters do not join in certain words. • **Practice Book:** Ask children to copy the words. • **Practice Book:** Ask children to copy the sentence.	• Settling routine • **Practice Book:** Ask children to copy the sentence. • **Practice Book:** Ask children to copy the words. • **Practice Book:** Ask the children to copy the sentence quickly.	• Settling routine • **Additional Practice sheet:** Ask children to copy the sentence. • **Additional Practice sheet:** Ask children to copy the joke neatly.
Assessment criterion	Can the child: – revise the break when letters don't join?	– practise the break when letters don't join?	– consolidate the break when letters don't join?
Further practice	To further practise break letters, you could ask children to: 1. write the word *you* ten times quickly without joining the *y* 2. write the word *gripping* ten times quickly without joining the *g* or *p*.		

Unit 15: Getting the height right: capital letters

	Lesson 1	Lesson 2	Practice
	Whole class seated at tables	*Class or groups seated at tables*	*Whole class or groups seated at tables*
Objective	To revise capital letters.	To practise capital letters.	To consolidate capital letters.
Resources	– Practice Book Page 17, Part 1 – Presentation Unit 15, Part 1 – Pencil or pen	– Practice Book Page 17, Part 2 – Presentation Unit 15, Part 2 – Pencil or pen	– Additional Practice sheet 15 – Presentation Unit 15, Part 3 – Pencil or pen
Teaching	• Settling routine and hand warm-up • Remind children to make sure that their capital letters are at the right height – just shorter than the tall letters. • **Practice Book:** Ask children to copy the sentence. • Use the **Presentation** to show the relative sizes of capital letters and other letters. • **Practice Book:** Ask children to copy the words. • **Practice Book:** Ask children to correct and copy the two sentences. Show the corrected version in the **Presentation**.	• Settling routine • **Practice Book:** Ask children to copy the alphabet in capital letters into their books. Remind them to make sure that they are just below the top line. You may wish to display it in the **Presentation**. • **Practice Book:** Ask children to correct and copy the sentence. Show the corrected version in the **Presentation**.	• Settling routine • **Additional Practice sheet:** Ask children to copy the sentence. • **Additional Practice sheet:** Ask children to correct the punctuation and capital letters and copy the sentences. Show the corrected version in the **Presentation**.
Assessment criterion	Can the student: – make the height of capital letters correct?	– make the height of capital letters correct?	– make the height of capital letters correct?
Further practice	To further practise getting the height of capital letters right, you could ask children to: 1. write the words *At All* and discuss the relative sizes of capital letters and *t* and tall letters 2. write the word *Stalk* ten times quickly with a capital *S*.		

Unit 16: Placing and spacing punctuation: commas and bullet points

	Lesson 1	**Lesson 2**	**Practice**
Objective	*Whole class seated at tables* To place and space commas.	*Class or groups seated at tables* To practise placing and spacing commas.	*Whole class or groups seated at tables* To consolidate placing and spacing commas.
Resources	– Practice Book Page 18, Part 1 – Presentation Unit 16, Part 1 – Pencil or pen	– Practice Book Page 18, Part 2 – Presentation Unit 16, Part 1 – Pencil or pen	– Additional Practice sheet 16 – Presentation Unit 16, Part 3 – Pencil or pen
Teaching	• Settling routine and hand warm-up • Tell children that, when commas are used, it changes the spacing of the words. • **Practice Book:** Ask children to copy the sentence. • **Practice Book:** Ask children to correct and copy the sentence. Show the corrected version in the **Presentation**.	• Settling routine • **Practice Book:** Ask children to copy the sentence. • **Practice Book:** Ask children to correct the capital letters, commas and full stop in the sentence, then copy it. Show the corrected version in the **Presentation**.	• Settling routine • **Additional Practice sheet:** Ask children to copy the sentence. • **Additional Practice sheet:** Ask children to complete the passage below, using items from the list, separated by commas. You may wish to display the passage in the **Presentation**.
Assessment criterion	Can the child: – recognise the difference between spacing when adding commas in lists?	– place and space commas correctly?	– place and space commas correctly?
Further practice	To further practise placing and spacing commas and using bullet points, you could ask children to: 1. write a sentence with items in a list, but no commas, then swap with a partner and correct each other's sentences 2. write a list of teachers in the school, using capital letters and commas 3. write a bullet-pointed list of the items in the **Additional Practice sheet** to remind Martha what to take on the school trip, or a bullet-pointed list of places they would like to visit.		

Unit 17: Writing direct speech

Lesson plan

	Lesson 1	Lesson 2	Practice
	Whole class seated at tables	*Class or groups seated at tables*	*Whole class or groups seated at tables*
Objective	To write direct speech neatly.	To practise writing direct speech neatly.	To consolidate writing direct speech neatly.
Resources	– Practice Book Page 19, Part 1 – Presentation Unit 17, Part 1 – Pencil or pen	– Practice Book Page 19, Part 2 – Presentation Unit 17, Part 2 – Pencil or pen	– Additional Practice sheet 17 – Presentation Unit 17, Part 3 – Pencil or pen
Teaching	• Settling routine and hand warm-up • Tell children that direct speech must be carefully structured and punctuated to clearly separate it from the rest of the text. Point out that each new line of direct speech should start with a capital letter. • **Practice Book:** Ask children to copy the words. • Use the **Presentation** to show the conversation, or ask children to look in their **Practice Book**. Ask children to copy the conversation neatly into their books.	• Settling routine • Use the **Presentation** to show the speech bubbles, or ask children to look in their **Practice Book**. Ask them to copy the direct speech into the sentences, adding speech marks, and then copy the completed sentences into their books.	• Settling routine • **Additional Practice sheet:** Ask children to copy the words. • **Additional Practice sheet:** Ask children to add the capital letters and speech marks, then copy the passage neatly into their books. Show the corrected version in the **Presentation**.
Assessment criterion	Can the student: – write direct speech accurately?	– write direct speech accurately?	– write direct speech accurately?
Further practice	To further practise writing direct speech, you could ask children to: 1. write a sentence that includes dialogue but no speech marks, then swap with a partner and correct each other's sentences 2. write a conversation between themselves and their best friend, using correct speech marks.		

Happy Handwriting

Unit 18: Placing and spacing: apostrophes

	Lesson 1	Lesson 2	Practice
	Whole class seated at tables	*Class or groups seated at tables*	*Whole class or groups seated at tables*
Objective	To place and space apostrophes.	To practise placing and spacing apostrophes.	To consolidate placing and spacing apostrophes.
Resources	– Practice Book Page 20, Part 1 – Presentation Unit 18, Part 1 – Pencil or pen	– Practice Book Page 20, Part 2 – Presentation Unit 18, Part 2 – Pencil or pen	– Additional Practice sheet 18 – Presentation Unit 18, Part 3 – Pencil or pen
Teaching	• **Settling routine and hand warm-up** • Tell children that, when replacing letters with an apostrophe, writers need to allow space for the apostrophe. • Use the **Presentation** to show the extra space needed for apostrophes. • **Practice Book:** Ask children to copy the words. • Use the **Presentation** to show the sentences, or ask children to look in their **Practice Book**. Ask children to correct and copy them. Show the corrected version in the **Presentation**.	• **Settling routine** • **Practice Book:** Ask children to copy the words. • Use the **Presentation** to show the sentence, or ask children to look in their **Practice Book**. Ask children to correct and copy it. Show the corrected version in the **Presentation**.	• **Settling routine** • **Additional Practice sheet:** Ask children to copy the sentence neatly. • **Additional Practice sheet:** Ask children to copy the words. • **Additional Practice sheet:** Ask children to change the underlined words into contractions and write the new sentence.
Assessment criterion	Can the child: – place and space apostrophes?	– place and space apostrophes?	– place and space apostrophes?
Further practice	To further practise placing and spacing apostrophes, you could ask children to: 1. write a sentence that includes contractions but no apostrophes, then swap with a partner and correct each other's sentences 2. write out *'she's, they'll, you've, he'd'* five times, making sure that the apostrophes are correct and adequately spaced.		

Lesson plan

Unit 19: Alphabetical order: to the second letter

	Lesson 1	Lesson 2	Practice
	Whole class seated at tables	*Class or groups seated at tables*	*Whole class or groups seated at tables*
Objective	To put words in alphabetical order.	To put words in alphabetical order.	To put words in alphabetical order.
Resources	– Practice Book Page 21, Part 1 – Presentation Unit 19, Part 1 – Pencil or pen	– Practice Book Page 21, Part 2 – Presentation Unit 19, Part 2 – Pencil or pen	– Additional Practice sheet 19 – Presentation Unit 19, Part 3 – Pencil or pen
Teaching	• Settling routine and hand warm-up • **Practice Book:** Ask children to copy the words. • **Practice Book:** Ask children to copy the list in alphabetical order, using the first and second letter of each item. Show the correct order in the **Presentation**.	• Settling routine • **Practice Book:** Ask children to copy the sentence. • **Practice Book:** Ask children to copy the list in alphabetical order, using the first and second letter of each item. Show the correct order in the **Presentation**.	• Settling routine • **Additional Practice sheet:** Ask children to copy the sentence. • **Additional Practice sheet:** Ask children to copy out the author names in alphabetical order. Remind children that if words start with the same first letter, they need to look at the second letter of each word. Show the correct order in the **Presentation**.
Assessment criterion	Can the child: – put words into alphabetical order using the first and second letter?	– put words into alphabetical order using the first and second letter?	– put words into alphabetical order using the first and second letter?
Further practice	To further practise alphabetical order, you could ask children to: 1. write out the alphabet so they can use it for reference 2. put the books in your classroom in alphabetical order.		

Happy Handwriting

Lesson plan

Unit 20: Self-assessment

	Lesson 1	Lesson 2	Lesson 3
Objective	*Whole class seated at tables*	*Class or groups seated at tables*	*Class or groups seated at tables*
	To self-assess handwriting.	To self-assess handwriting.	To self-assess handwriting.
Resources	– Practice Book Page 22, Part 1 – Presentation Unit 20, Part 1 – Pencil or pen	– Practice Book Page 22, Part 2 – Presentation Unit 20, Part 2 – Pencil or pen	– Paper or exercise book – Pencil or pen
Teaching	• **Settling routine and hand warm-up** • Have a discussion in class to remind children of the criteria for good handwriting (see page 20). • Use the **Presentation** to show the passage, or ask children to look in their **Practice Book.** Ask children to correct the capital letters and punctuation, then copy the passage neatly. Show the corrected version in the **Presentation.** • Use the **Presentation** to model how to assess their writing.	• **Settling routine** • Use the **Presentation** to show the sentences, or ask children to look in their **Practice Book.** Ask children to correct the capital letters and punctuation, then copy the sentences quickly. They should time themselves to see how long it takes. Show the corrected version in the **Presentation.** • Use the **Presentation** to model how to assess their writing.	• **Settling routine** • Children look through their independent writing and self-assess by completing the following sentences: This term I have improved _____. I need to practise _____.
Assessment criterion	Can the child: – assess their own handwriting?	– assess their own handwriting?	– complete the following sentences? This term I have improved _____. I need to practise _____.
Further practice	To further practise their handwriting, you could ask children to: 1. write a list, using commas or bullet points, of things they'd like for their birthday 2. write a conversation between two friends about their weekend plans, using speech marks and contractions appropriately.		

Lesson plan

Unit 21: Writing notes quickly

	Lesson 1	Lesson 2	Practice
	Whole class seated at tables	*Class or groups seated at tables*	*Whole class or groups seated at tables*
Objective	To write notes quickly.	To write notes quickly.	To write notes quickly.
Resources	– Practice Book Page 23, Part 1 – Presentation Unit 21, Part 1 – Pencil or pen	– Practice Book Page 23, Part 2 – Presentation Unit 21, Part 2 – Pencil or pen	– Additional Practice sheet 21 – Presentation Unit 21, Part 3 – Pencil or pen
Teaching	• Settling routine and hand warm-up • **Practice Book:** Ask children to copy the words. • **Practice Book:** Ask children to read the passage, underline two key points and then write them out quickly.	• Settling routine • **Practice Book:** Ask children to copy the words. • **Practice Book:** Ask children to read the passage, underline two key points and then write them out quickly.	• Settling routine • **Additional Practice sheet:** Ask children to copy the sentence neatly. • **Additional Practice sheet:** Ask children to underline the key points and write some quick notes about the passage.
Assessment criterion	Can the child: – write out key points quickly?	– write out key points quickly?	– write out key points quickly?
Further practice	To further practise making notes, you could ask children to: 1. make notes about a book they are reading 2. watch and make notes about a video.		

Happy Handwriting

Lesson plan

Unit 22: Joining to and from *k*

	Lesson 1	Lesson 2	Practice
	Whole class seated at tables	*Class or groups seated at tables*	*Whole class or groups seated at tables*
Objective	To consolidate joins to and from *k*.	To practise joining *k*.	To practise joining *k*.
Resources	– Practice Book Page 24, Part 1 – Presentation Unit 22, Part 1 – Pencil or pen	– Practice Book Page 24, Part 2 – Presentation Unit 22, Part 2 – Pencil or pen	– Additional Practice sheet 22 – Presentation Unit 22, Part 3 – Pencil or pen
Teaching	• **Settling routine and hand warm-up** • Point out that the diagonal join from *k* to the next letter is unusual. • Use the **Presentation** to show the joins in the words. • **Practice Book:** Ask children to copy the words. • Use the **Presentation** to show the sentences, or ask children to look in their **Practice Book**. Ask children to copy the sentences.	• **Settling routine** • **Practice Book:** Ask children to copy the words. • Use the **Presentation** to show the joins in: *icket, acket, ucket, ocket*. Ask children to copy them. • Use the **Presentation** to show the activity, or ask children to look in their **Practice Book:** • Ask children to trace over and match the first letters with the correct endings to make four words. Show how the first one has been done for them as an example. Children should then write a sentence for each word.	• **Settling routine** • **Additional Practice sheet:** Ask children to copy the sentence. • **Additional Practice sheet:** Ask children to copy the passage neatly.
Assessment criterion	Can the child: – join to and from *k*?	– join to and from *k*?	– join to and from *k*?
Further practice	To further practice joining to and from *k*, you could ask children to: 1. write out these target words on plain paper/cards, making sure the joins are correct: *cricket, pocket, racket* 2. pick two words with joins to and from *k* that they have written in this unit, and write two sentences using these words.		

Happy Handwriting

Unit 23: Revising key joins: joins to round letters

	Lesson 1	Lesson 2	Practice
	Whole class seated at tables	*Class or groups seated at tables*	*Whole class or groups seated at tables*
Objective	To revise joins to round letters.	To practise joins to round letters.	To consolidate joins to round letters.
Resources	– Practice Book Page 25, Part 1 – Presentation Unit 23, Part 1 – Pencil or pen	– Practice Book Page 25, Part 2 – Presentation Unit 23, Part 2 – Pencil or pen	– Additional Practice sheet 23 – Presentation Unit 23, Part 3 – Pencil or pen
Teaching	• Settling routine and hand warm-up • **Practice Book:** Ask children to copy the words. • Use the **Presentation** to show the passage, or ask children to look in their **Practice Book**. Ask children to copy the passage.	• Settling routine • **Practice Book:** Ask children to copy the words. • Use the **Presentation** to show the sentence, or ask children to look in their **Practice Book**: Ask children to use the words above to complete the sentences, then copy them.	• Settling routine • **Additional Practice sheet:** Ask children to copy the sentence quickly. • **Additional Practice sheet:** Ask children to copy the account quickly.
Assessment criterion	Can the child: – join to round letters?	– join to round letters?	– join to round letters?
Further practice	To further practise joining to and from round letters, you could ask children to: 1. turn these into past-tense words by adding -ed: *walk, play, decide, age, paint* 2. Then write an account using these past-tense words: *walked, played, decided, aged, painted, rode.*		

Unit 24: Getting the height right

	Lesson 1	Lesson 2	Practice
	Whole class seated at tables	*Class or groups seated at tables*	*Whole class or groups seated at tables*
Objective	To practise *ial*.	To practise *ial*.	To consolidate *ial*.
Resources	– Practice Book Page 26, Part 1 – Presentation Unit 24, Part 1 – Pencil or pen	– Practice Book Page 26, Part 2 – Presentation Unit 24, Part 2 – Pencil or pen	– Additional Practice sheet 24 – Presentation Unit 24, Part 3 – Pencil or pen
Teaching	• **Settling routine and hand warm-up** • Remind children to keep ascenders tall and parallel. • Use the **Presentation** to show the relative sizes of letters. • **Practice Book:** Ask children to copy the words. • Use the **Presentation** to show the sentences, or ask children to look in their **Practice Book**. Ask children to copy the sentences neatly.	• **Settling routine** • Use the **Presentation** to show the sentence. Point out the sizes of all the tall letters. Ask children to copy the sentence. • **Practice Book:** Ask children to copy the words. • Use the **Presentation** to show the passage, or ask children to look in their **Practice Book**. Ask children to copy the passage neatly.	• **Settling routine** • **Additional Practice sheet:** Ask children to copy the sentence. • Use the **Presentation** to show the acrostic poem, or ask children to look at their **Additional Practice sheet**. Ask children to copy the poem into their books.
Assessment criterion	Can the child: – write tall letters at the correct height?	– write tall letters at the correct height?	– write tall letters at the correct height?
Further practice	To further practise getting the height of tall letters right, you could ask children to: 1. write the words *at all* and discuss the relative sizes of tall letters 2. write the word *chalk* ten times quickly.		

Lesson plan

Unit 25: Printing and labelling

	Lesson 1	Lesson 2	Practice
	Whole class seated at tables	*Class or groups seated at tables*	*Whole class or groups seated at tables*
Objective	To print in unjoined letters and to label.	To print in unjoined letters and to label.	To print in unjoined letters and to label.
Resources	– Practice Book Page 27, Part 1 – Presentation Unit 25, Part 1 – Pencil or pen	– Practice Book Page 27, Part 2 – Presentation Unit 25, Part 2 – Pencil or pen	– Additional Practice sheet 25 – Presentation Unit 25, Part 3 – Pencil or pen
Teaching	• Settling routine and hand warm-up • Tell children that people often print labels and addresses in unjoined capital letters so they can be read clearly. Postcodes are always written in printed capital letters. Addresses should be left-aligned. • **Practice Book:** Ask children to copy the words. • Use the **Presentation** to show the addresses, or ask children to look in their **Practice Book**. Ask children to copy the addresses into their books, left-aligning them and using printed capital letters for the postcodes.	• Settling routine • **Practice Book:** Ask children to copy the sentence. • Use the **Presentation** to show the addresses, or ask children to look in their **Practice Book**. Ask children to correct the addresses and write them into their books, neatly and with the correct alignment.	• Settling routine • **Additional Practice sheet:** Ask children to copy the sentence. • Use the **Presentation** to show the address, or ask children to look at their **Additional Practice sheet**. Ask children to copy the address neatly.
Assessment criterion	**Can the child:** – print in unjoined capitals and write addresses neatly?	– print in unjoined capitals and write addresses neatly?	– print in unjoined capitals and write addresses neatly?
Further practice	To further practise printing capital letters, you could ask children to: 1. address an envelope or write a letter to a friend, including their own address and their friend's address 2. prepare a set of labels for drawers or containers in the classroom.		

Happy Handwriting

Lesson plan

Unit 26: Placing and spacing punctuation: speech marks

	Lesson 1	Lesson 2	Practice
	Whole class seated at tables	*Class or groups seated at tables*	*Whole class or groups seated at tables*
Objective	To place and space speech marks.	To practise placing and spacing speech marks.	To consolidate placing and spacing speech marks.
Resources	– Practice Book Page 28, Part 1 – Presentation Unit 26, Part 1 – Pencil or pen	– Practice Book Page 28, Part 2 – Presentation Unit 26, Part 2 – Pencil or pen	– Additional Practice sheet 26 – Presentation Unit 26, Part 3 – Pencil or pen
Teaching	• Settling routine and hand warm-up • Tell children that speech marks change the spacing between words. • **Practice Book:** Ask children to copy the sentence. • Use the **Presentation** to show the sentences, or ask children to look in their **Practice Book**. Ask children to correct the speech marks and capital letters, then copy the sentences. Show the corrected version in the **Presentation** and point out how the speech marks and capital letters have changed the spacings.	• Settling routine • **Practice Book:** Ask children to copy the sentence. • Use the **Presentation** to show the sentences, or ask children to look in their **Practice Book.** Ask children to correct the speech marks and capital letters, then copy the sentences. Show the corrected version in the **Presentation** and point out how the speech marks and capital letters have changed the spacings.	• Settling routine • **Additional Practice sheet:** Ask children to copy the sentence. • Use the **Presentation** to show the sentences, or ask children to look at their **Additional Practice sheet.** Ask children to correct the speech marks and capital letters. Remind them to start a new line for a new speaker. Then ask them to copy the sentences. Show the corrected version in the **Presentation** and point out how each new speaker starts on a new line.
Assessment criterion	Can the child: – recognise the difference between spacing when adding speech marks?	– place and space speech marks correctly?	– place and space speech marks correctly, starting a new line for a new speaker?
Further practice	To further practise placing and spacing speech marks, you could ask children to: 1. write some dialogue with no speech marks or capital letters, then swap with a partner and correct each other's sentences 2. copy out some text from a book that includes speech marks.		

Happy Handwriting

Unit 27: Writing quickly: words per minute

	Lesson 1	Lesson 2	Practice
	Whole class seated at tables	*Class or groups seated at tables*	*Whole class or groups seated at tables*
Objective	To write quickly.	To write quickly.	To write quickly.
Resources	– Practice Book Page 29, Part 1 – Presentation Unit 27, Part 1 – Pencil or pen	– Practice Book Page 29, Part 2 – Presentation Unit 27, Part 2 – Pencil or pen	– Additional Practice sheet 27 – Presentation Unit 27, Part 3 – Pencil or pen
Teaching	• Settling routine and hand warm-up • Before you begin, emphasise the need to make fast writing legible, not rushed. • Use the **Presentation** to show the passage, or ask children to look in their **Practice Book**. Ask children to copy the passage quickly into their books and time themselves. How long did it take them to write 23 readable words?	• Settling routine • Use the **Presentation** to show the facts, or ask children to look in their **Practice Book**. Ask children to copy the facts quickly into their books and time themselves. How long did it take them to write 45 readable words?	• Settling routine • **Additional Practice sheet:** Ask children to copy the sentence quickly. • Use the **Presentation** to show the passage, or ask children to look at their **Additional Practice sheet**. Ask the children to copy the passage quickly into their books.
Assessment criterion	Can the child: – write quickly?	– write quickly?	– write out key points quickly?
Further practice	To further practise making notes, you could ask children to: 1. make notes on their reading books 2. make notes on a video.		

Unit 28: Writing neatly: a formal letter

	Lesson 1	Lesson 2	Practice
	Whole class seated at tables	*Class or groups seated at tables*	*Whole class or groups seated at tables*
Objective	To write neatly.	To write neatly.	To write neatly.
Resources	– Practice Book Page 30, Part 1 – Presentation Unit 28, Part 1 – Pencil or pen	– Practice Book Page 30, Part 2 – Presentation Unit 28, Part 2 – Pencil or pen	– Additional Practice sheet 28 – Presentation Unit 28, Part 3 – Pencil or pen
Teaching	• Settling routine and hand warm-up • Remind children that they should choose to write neatly when they know their reader will appreciate it. • **Practice Book**: Ask children to copy the words. • Use the **Presentation** to show the passage, or ask children to look in their **Practice Book**. Ask children to copy the passage neatly into their books.	• Settling routine • **Practice Book**: Ask children to copy the words neatly. • Use the **Presentation** to show the words, or ask children to look in their **Practice Book**. Ask children to use the words to help them write a polite complaint in their books, using their best handwriting.	• Settling routine • **Additional Practice sheet**: Ask children to copy the sentence. • Use the **Presentation** to show the message, or ask children to look at their **Additional Practice sheet**. Ask children to add the correct punctuation and capital letters and copy the message in their best handwriting. Show the corrected version in the **Presentation**.
Assessment criterion	Can the child: – write neatly?	– write neatly?	– write neatly?
Further practice	To further practise writing neatly, you could ask children to: 1. write a polite letter to their local councillor to complain about an issue that affects their community 2. write '*I would like a replacement*' three times, then analyse which attempt is best and why.		

Unit 29: Spacing items in a list

	Lesson 1	Lesson 2	Practice
	Whole class seated at tables	*Class or groups seated at tables*	*Whole class or groups seated at tables*
Objective	To place and space items in a list.	To practise placing and spacing items in a list.	To consolidate placing and spacing items in a list.
Resources	– Practice Book Page 31, Part 1 – Presentation Unit 29, Part 1 – Pencil or pen	– Practice Book Page 31, Part 2 – Presentation Unit 29, Part 2 – Pencil or pen	– Additional Practice sheet 29 – Presentation Unit 29, Part 3 – Pencil or pen
Teaching	• **Settling routine and hand warm-up** • Point out that commas or bullet points need extra spacing. • **Practice Book:** Ask children to copy the sentence. • Use the **Presentation** to show the passage, or ask children to look in their **Practice Book**. Ask children to add commas to the list, then copy the sentence. Show the corrected version in the **Presentation**.	• **Settling routine** • Use the **Presentation** to show the sentence, or ask children to look in their **Practice Book**. Ask children to change the sentence into a bullet-pointed list. Show the corrected version in the **Presentation**.	• **Settling routine** • **Additional Practice sheet:** Ask children to copy the sentence. • Use the **Presentation** to show the passage, or ask children to look at their **Additional Practice sheet**. Ask children to add commas to the list. Show the corrected version in the **Presentation**. • Now ask children to change the sentence into a bullet-pointed list. They may need some support with this – for example, guide children to start with the stem 'On her trip, Maryam took:' and point out that they don't need the final 'and' in a bullet-pointed list. Show the corrected version in the **Presentation**.
Assessment criterion	Can the child: – place and space commas and bullet points correctly?	– place and space commas and bullet points correctly?	– place and space commas and bullet points correctly?
Further practice	To further practise placing and spacing items in a list, you could ask children to: 1. write some lists of items with no commas, then swap with a partner to correct each other's lists and/or turn them into bullet-pointed lists 2. write a list of teachers in the school, using bullet points.		

Unit 30: Self-assessment

	Lesson 1	Lesson 2	Lesson 3
	Whole class seated at tables	*Class or groups seated at tables*	*Class or groups seated at tables*
Objective	To self-assess handwriting.	To self-assess handwriting.	To self-assess handwriting.
Resources	– Practice Book Page 32, Part 1 – Presentation Unit 30, Part 1 – Pencil or pen	– Practice Book Page 32, Part 2 – Presentation Unit 30, Part 2 – Pencil or pen	– Paper or exercise book – Pencil or pen
Teaching	• **Settling routine and hand warm-up** • Have a discussion in class to remind children of the criteria for good handwriting (see page 20). • Use the **Presentation** to show the sentences, or ask children to look in their **Practice Book**. Ask children to correct the capital letters and punctuation, then copy the sentences neatly. Show the corrected version in the **Presentation**. • Use the **Presentation** to model how to assess their writing.	• **Settling routine** • Use the **Presentation** to show the sentences, or ask children to look in their **Practice Book**. Ask children to correct the capital letters and punctuation, then copy the sentences quickly. They should time themselves to see how long it takes. Show the corrected version in the **Presentation**. • Use the **Presentation** to model how to assess their writing.	• **Settling routine** • Children look through their independent writing and self-assess by completing the following sentences: This term I have improved _____. I need to practise _____.
	Can the child:		
Assessment criterion	– assess their own handwriting?	– assess their own handwriting?	– complete the following sentences? This term I have improved _____. I need to practise _____.
Further practice	To further practise their handwriting, you could ask children to: 1. write a formal letter to someone they admire, explaining why they look up to them 2. work in pairs, with one child describing what their bedroom is like and the other making notes as quickly as possible.		

Name: _____   Unit 1: **Writing quickly and writing neatly**

✏ Copy the sentence neatly.

It is important to be able to write quickly and neatly.

✏ Copy the words quickly.

and					too

because				if

✏ Copy the passage into your book in your neatest handwriting.

Neat handwriting helps the reader to understand your message. You might need to use particularly neat handwriting to write an invitation or a card.

--✂

Name: _____   Unit 2: *Joining to and from e*

✏ Write as quickly as you can.

de					fe

en					ce

✏ Fill in the missing words and copy the sentence neatly.

My dog is extremely _____, but he sometimes barks to _____ me.
(obedient / defend)

Happy Handwriting 5: Additional practice sheet			© HarperCollinsPublishers Ltd. 2022

Name: _____   Unit 3: *Joining to and from r*

✏️ Copy the sentence.

Take care when writing r.

✏️ Copy the words quickly.

share

prepare

fanfare

✏️ Copy the words neatly.

share   prepare   fanfare

--✂

Name: _____   Unit 4: *Revising key joins: diagonal joins*

✏️ Copy the sentence.

Some diagonal joins go to tall letters.

✏️ Copy the words quickly.

tall, taller, tallest

small, smaller, smallest

big, bigger, biggest

✏️ Copy the question into your book, then answer it.

If Sami is taller than Jake, and Petra is smaller than Jake, who is the tallest?

Happy Handwriting 5: Additional practice sheet   © HarperCollinsPublishers Ltd. 2022

Name: _____ Unit 5: *Ascenders and descenders*

Copy the sentence.

The letters 'ough' make many different sounds.

Copy the passage. Make sure that the capitals and tall letters are correct.

Sasha has had enough! Spelling words with 'ough' is so tough. She ought to be an expert after practising, though.

Name: _____ Unit 6: *Punctuation in sentences*

Copy the sentence.

Use a full stop, question mark or exclamation mark at the end of a sentence.

Copy the exclamations.

Help! Oh no! Sorry!

Correct the punctuation and capital letters, then copy the passage into your book.

hi jared where is your favourite place in london i love buckingham palace

Name: _____   Unit 7: *Writing quickly*

Copy the sentence quickly.

Practice makes perfect!

See how quickly you can write these notes as full sentences.
- Buy hat
- Book train
- Pack suncream

Name: _____   Unit 8: *Writing neatly*

Copy the sentence neatly.

Neat writing takes slightly longer.

Correct the punctuation and capital letters, then copy the passage in your best handwriting.

thank you for inviting me to your party I had the best time will you be able to come to mine next week

Name: _____

Unit 9: **Alphabetical order**

Copy the sentence neatly.

Alphabetical order is very useful.

Copy out the list, in alphabetical order. Remember that if words start with the same first letter, you need to look at the second letter of each word.

cake, sandwiches, fruit, cheese, crisps, sweets

Name: _____ Unit 11: *Joining to and from t*

Copy out the sentence neatly.

It is interesting to join the letter t.

Copy out the sentence in your neatest handwriting.

In the interview, we want you to talk to the interviewer without interrupting them.

Name: _____ Unit 12: *Joining to and from f*

Copy out the sentence neatly.

It is useful to join f carefully.

Complete the table.

help	helpful	helpfully
use		usefully
	dreadful	
care		

Happy Handwriting 5: Additional practice sheet © HarperCollinsPublishers Ltd. 2022

Name: _____   Unit 13: *Revising key joins: horizontal joins*

✏️ Copy the words quickly.

lovely

lively

wearily

wonky

✏️ Copy the poem into your book, in your neatest handwriting.

I love to live bravely.

You live to love bravely.

We both walk bravely.

Bravely as we live and love.

Name: _____   Unit 14: *Revising break letters: y, j, g, p*

✏️ Copy the sentence.

Letters with 'tails' do not join.

✏️ Copy the joke neatly.

Why did the golfer wear two gloves?

In case he got a hole in one!

Name: _____   Unit 15: *Getting the height right: capital letters*

✏ Copy the sentence.

Capital letters are slightly shorter than tall letters.

✏ Correct the capital letters, then copy the sentences.

Asif had never been to new york before. he was looking forward to seeing times square.

- ✂

Name: _____   Unit 16: *Commas and bullet points*

✏ Copy the sentence.

Remember to add commas between items in a list.

✏ Complete the passage, using words from the following list. Separate the words with commas.

Items for school trip:

| pencil | lunchbox | notebook | water |

Martha took her _____ _____ _____ and _____ on the school trip.

Happy Handwriting 5: Additional practice sheet   © HarperCollinsPublishers Ltd. 2022

Name: _____ Unit 17: **Writing direct speech**

✏️ Copy the words.

yelped

shouted

breathed

✏️ Add capital letters and speech marks to the passage. Then copy it neatly into your book.

the shop is over there, I think, ruth said.

Are you sure? said niall

It doesn't look like a shop to me snorted hamid

well, we can go and look around suggested niall

Name: _____ Unit 18: **Apostrophes**

✏️ Copy the sentence neatly.

Informal writing often uses contractions.

✏️ Copy the words.

who's _____ what's _____ how's _____

✏️ Change the underlined words into contractions, then write the new sentence.

<u>Who is</u> your friend?   Who's your friend?

<u>When is</u> your birthday?

<u>What is</u> your name?

<u>How is</u> your grandma?

Happy Handwriting 5: Additional practice sheet   © HarperCollinsPublishers Ltd. 2022

Name: _____   Unit 19: **Alphabetical order: to the second letter**

Copy the sentence neatly.

Alphabetical order is very useful for finding books in a library.

Copy out these surnames in alphabetical order. Remember that if words start with the same first letter, you need to look at the second letter of each word.

Morpurgo, Milne, Donaldson, Dahl, Digby, Potter, Pullman

Name: _____   Unit 21: **Writing notes quickly**

✏️ *Copy the sentence neatly.*

Notes do not have to be in full sentences.

✏️ *Underline the key points in the passage. Write some quick notes about them.*

Sadly, lions are only found in isolated areas because of illegal hunting and habitat destruction. We must conserve lion habitats so they can thrive.

-- ✂

Name: _____   Unit 22: **Joining to and from k**

✏️ *Copy the sentence neatly.*

It is important to join k accurately.

✏️ *Copy the passage neatly.*

If I were king for a day, I would be keen to make the world a kinder place. I would keep reminding people that kindness is key.

Name: _____   Unit 23: **Revising key joins: joins to round letters**

Copy the sentence quickly.

Remember not to join from p.

Copy the passage quickly.

We walked along the South Bank to the Tate art gallery. We looked at the paintings with interest and visited the gift shop at the end.

Name: _____   Unit 24: **Getting the height right**

Copy the sentence.

Letter height is important.

Copy the acrostic poem into your book.

Tall letters are not small.
All tall letters must stand tall.
Little letters stand small but
Letters that are tall stand tall.

Happy Handwriting 5: Additional practice sheet   © HarperCollinsPublishers Ltd. 2022

Name: _____   Unit 25: *Printing and labelling*

✏️ Copy the sentence.

Addresses should be left-aligned.

✏️ Copy the address neatly.

Madeline Mckirby
80 Dribel Road
Southampton
SOU4 5TG

--✂️

Name: _____   Unit 26: *Speech marks*

✏️ Copy the sentence.

Start a new line for a new speaker.

✏️ Add capital letters and speech marks to the sentences, then copy the sentences. Remember to start a new line for a new speaker.

we will be in big trouble if we are late ajay said it'll be fine responded letty don't be a baby

Name: _____   Unit 27: *Writing quickly: words per minute*

✏ Copy the sentence quickly.

Speed writing is a useful skill.

✏ Copy the passage quickly into your book.

A clock is a device that tells us the time. There are two types: analogue and digital. Most electrical items show the digital time. Analogue clocks are typically circular, and have numbers around the edge and moving hands.

-- ✂

Name: _____   Unit 28: *Writing neatly: a formal letter*

✏ Copy the sentence neatly.

Neat writing takes slightly longer.

✏ Add the correct punctuation and capital letters to the passage. Then copy it in your neatest handwriting.

i am writing to say thank you for the generous gift we will think of you when we use it on our holiday.

Name: _____   Unit 29: *Spacing items in a list*

Copy the sentence.

You can use commas or bullet points to show items in a list.

Add commas to the list.

Maryam took a two-person tent a camping stove a cosy sleeping bag and a wind-up torch on her trip.

Now rewrite the sentence above using bullet points.

Happy Handwriting 5: Additional practice sheet © HarperCollinsPublishers Ltd. 2022

Assessing handwriting in Year 5

There are a number of types of assessment of handwriting:

- statutory summative assessment – to compare pupil performance with national expectations and comparisons
- day-to-day formative assessment – to inform teaching on an ongoing basis
- diagnostic assessment to identify particular strengths and weaknesses
- in-school summative assessment – to understand pupil performance at the end of a period of teaching.

Assessing handwriting in the National Curriculum – the end of Key Stage 2

Teacher assessment

At the end of Key Stage 2, teachers must assess using the Teacher Assessment Frameworks. These holistic assessments include the following handwriting requirements:

- Working towards the expected standard: The pupil can write legibly, although not necessarily in a joined hand.
- Working at the expected standard: The pupil maintains legibility in joined handwriting when writing at speed.

The National Curriculum states that pupils should be taught to 'write legibly, fluently and with increasing speed by choosing which shape of a letter to use when given choices and deciding whether or not to join specific letters; choosing the writing implement that is best suited for a task.'

These goals are also the basis of in-school summative assessment, which may be informed by your day-to-day assessments of handwriting and the children's self-assessment at the end of each term.

Day-to-day assessment of handwriting in your class in Year 5

To make an overall assessment of children's handwriting in Year 5, it is important to consider both the product of their writing and the way they do the writing. We suggest that comprehensive assessment of handwriting in Year 5 includes:

- scrutiny of a child's written notes, or informal writing, written at some speed
- scrutiny of a child's final draft or presentation writing.

The handwriting example record sheet on page 66 will support your assessment by providing key considerations and a point scale for each item.

Fluent, legible and speedy handwriting in Year 5 is based on correct letter formation and correct joining between letters. To know whether children have formed a letter or join correctly, you need to see them do it.

Observation of the act of writing is vital, especially where children are struggling. Observe handwriting while children are using the Practice Book and also in children's free writing.

A general assessment record sheet for handwriting (Year 5) is on page 67 of this guide. In Year 5, you may also want to record which letter formations children can use and which ones require more practice. An assessment record sheet for letter formations, to be used particularly with children who may still require additional handwriting practice, is in the printable resources for Year 5.

The use of joins should be becoming automatic in Year 5, but for a few children this will remain a challenging goal. Facilitating this will enable the children to compose what they want to say more freely, so it is worth the effort to arrange additional practice. An assessment record sheet for joins between letters in Year 5 is on page 68 of this guide. In addition, the *Happy Handwriting* resources in this guide include more detailed assessment and practice materials, which you will find useful for children who need particular handwriting support:

- Year 5 speed and fluency practice sheets for the formation of letter families
- Year 5 extra practice sheets for diagonal joins, horizontal joins and joins to round letters.

Self-assessment of handwriting

Understanding the criteria for 'good' handwriting is very important, and these criteria change as children go through their education. In Year 5, all children should be able to form all letters correctly and be secure in forming joins. Size, orientation and spacing of letters should be largely under control, and children are learning to choose whether to write quickly or with full attention to neatness. In either case, writers should aim for legible text.

Talking about these criteria during handwriting lessons is important, and the full glossary in the printable resources will be useful. Whenever children complete handwriting practice, it is a good idea to ask them to consider how well they achieved their handwriting goals and to identify what they still find difficult in handwriting. The units in Weeks 10, 20 and 30 are designed to support children to self-evaluate their handwriting. You could also ask children to consider their writing in another context, to evaluate how much of their success at handwriting lessons is evident.

Diagnostic assessment of handwriting

A small proportion of children in Year 5 will benefit from a more in-depth assessment of their handwriting to enable them to make progress. When you have identified which aspects of handwriting are particularly challenging for individuals or groups, you will be able to use the *Happy Handwriting* materials to provide additional practice for these children.

At Year 5, automatic and correct formation of letters remains vital, and is an underlying priority for all children if they are to write legibly, but a few children may still struggle with this. Joining letters automatically is the next most important priority. Other aspects of effective handwriting, identified in the assessment guidance above, include spacing and speed. These aspects of handwriting are dependent on good, automatic formation and joining. You can assess the handwriting of children who appear to be struggling diagnostically and offer individuals or groups of children additional practice to help them to improve a particular aspect of their handwriting. This will help them become automatic in their writing and reduce the attention they have to give this basic aspect of their learning.

Use the diagnostic assessment of handwriting sheet (page 69) and the instructions below to do a diagnostic assessment. The assessment should be done in small groups, with an adult who can give clear instructions and observe the letter formation that children use as they complete the sheet. The Year 5 diagnostic assessment of handwriting sheet (page 69) includes three short tasks: copying some sentences, a free writing task, and writing out the alphabet from memory. Observe these tasks and decide whether each child can:

- form letters correctly and consistently, without hesitation, when they copy the sentences
- form letters correctly and consistently, without hesitation, when they write a sentence they are composing themselves

- join the letters correctly and consistently in the copying task and composing task (noting which joins they use)
- write out the lower-case alphabet from memory at least once, without hesitation, within a minute.

Until children in Year 5 are able to produce letters automatically, they will struggle to join letters or write quickly. For some children, joining letters will always be difficult. In Year 5, you may need to choose a particular focus for handwriting practice. If a struggling writer is having difficulty with automatic letter production and joining letters, it is most important that they can produce the letters automatically and consistently. This should remain the most basic handwriting priority because it will help them most with their composition.

The additional practice activities and targeted sheets in this Teacher's Guide, the further practice suggestions in each week's lesson plan, and the printable resources offer plenty of opportunities for you to help children practise the aspects of handwriting that they need to develop further.

Instructions for diagnostic assessment

The copying task

Ask the children to copy the sentences as quickly and legibly as they can, onto the sheet. Observe them as they do this. Identify any letters that the child writes incorrectly or inconsistently, or that cause the child to hesitate before writing. These letters need to be learned more thoroughly as a movement. Observe which joins are used, and which of these are incorrect and/or cause the child to pause.

The extra practice sheets in the printable resources can be used to support improvement in letter formation. We recommend practice focused on the letters causing difficulty rather than repeating all the letters. The speed and fluency practice sheets on pages 74–76 should be used to promote automatic letter production.

The free writing task

Ask the children to compose a piece of writing about their dream holiday, in an exercise book or on paper. Consider how much they write as part of the assessment.

It is important to observe free writing because you should aim to be sure that, when composing text, children still maintain efficient handwriting when other parts of the writing process demand attention. Again, the aim is to identify any letters or joins that children form incorrectly or inconsistently, or that cause children to hesitate (a sure sign that the movement is not automatic).

The free writing and copying tasks should be completed within 15 minutes. If children can only produce a few words, this suggests that they need more letter production practice to improve their handwriting speed. The speed and fluency practice sheets (pages 74–76) can be useful for very slow writers.

The alphabet writing task – automatic letter production

Ask children to: Please write out the letters of the alphabet, in lower case, as quickly and neatly as possible. If you complete writing the alphabet, start again until I say 'stop'.

Give the children one minute to write the alphabet, then say 'stop'.

This is an activity to test how quickly the children can produce a well-known sequence of letters (the alphabet) so it is only useful if they know the alphabet reasonably well. We would expect all children to be able to write out the alphabet in less than a minute by the start of Year 3, and in Year 5 we would expect them to be able to do so neatly and legibly.

If children struggle to produce letters automatically, use the speed and fluency practice sheets (pages 74–76) to improve automatic letter production. These activities work by asking children to repeatedly write unpredictable combinations of letters. The unusual combinations of letters mean that the children have to repeatedly bring each letter formation to mind, which helps to fix it in their memory.

Activities to promote automatic letter production

The speed and fluency practice sheets (pages 74–76) aim to promote automatic writing of letters without children having to actively think about the letter movement. Where children cannot yet write letters in this way, the traditional practice of writing out rows of the same letters or predictable letter combinations does not help very much. To improve automatic writing of letters, children should practise unlikely and unexpected combinations of letters, which force them to 'bring to mind' the letter shape and movement quickly. You can use some simple school equipment to do a small number of activities that help children practise this. These activities are best done with groups of children in short, intense sessions.

You will need:

- a timing device for one, two and three minutes
- spinners, magnetic letters
- alphabet letter cards (from the printable resources)
- paper and pencil.

Letter spinner: One child is the 'timer' and one child is the 'spinner' in each round. The 'spinner' spins two or three letter spinners and calls out the letter names. The 'timer' starts a timer for one minute. The rest of the children have to write out the letters 'called', as a sequence, as many times as they can in one minute. Children should say the letters' names as they write them. This helps children to fix the letter movement and name in their memory.

Feelie bag letters: One child is the 'timer' and one child is the 'drawerer' in each round. The 'drawerer' pulls two or three letters out of a bag (or box) and calls out the letter names. The 'timer' starts a timer for one minute. The rest of the children have to write out the letters 'called' as many times as they can in one minute, saying the letter name as they write it. This helps children to fix the letter movement and name in their memory.

Letter cards: One child is the 'timer' and one child is the 'dealer' in each round. The 'dealer' deals three letter cards and says their names aloud. The 'timer' starts a timer for one minute. The rest of the children in the group have to write that combination of letters as many times as they can in one minute. This helps children to fix the visual representation of the letter in their minds.

Handwriting example record sheet

Child name	Sits appropriately with feet and shoulders straight	Starts letters at the right place	Makes the correct letter movement without hesitation	Consistently uses the correct letter movement wherever the letter occurs	Keeps the pencil on the paper between joined letters	Writes short letters, ascenders and descenders in the correct proportions	Makes target joins between letters in the Practice Book	Uses target joins in their own writing	Knows the names and order of letters in the alphabet
1									
2									
3									
4									
5									
6									
7									
8									
9									
10									
11									
12									
13									
14									
15									
16									
17									
18									
19									
20									
21									
22									
23									
24									
25									
26									
27									
28									
29									
30									

Assessment record sheet for Year 5 handwriting

Child's name	Legibility (5 = easily read, 1 = unable to read)	Regular in size and spacing (5 = very regular, 1 = very erratic)	Flow in the joining (5 = well joined flow, 1 = no joins)	Letter height and joins are consistent (5 = very consistent, 1 = very erratic)	Letters and words are appropriate in size and position (5 = all relatively appropriate, 1 = very varied)	Total
1						
2						
3						
4						
5						
6						
7						
8						
9						
10						
11						
12						
13						
14						
15						
16						
17						
18						
19						
20						
21						
22						
23						
24						
25						
26						
27						
28						
29						
30						

Happy Handwriting

Assessment record sheet for joins in Year 5

Name/group name: Date:

Can the child?	Diagonal joins to letters without ascenders	Diagonal joins to letters with ascenders	Horizontal joins to letters without ascenders	Horizontal joins to letters with ascenders	Joins to round (anti-clockwise) letters
	Diagonal join to short letter	Diagonal join to tall letter	Horizontal join to short letter	Horizontal join to tall letter	Joins to round letters
	im re an ra	*ake th all ef*	*or wa fa ve*	*wh ot vl*	*ed ing ra*
Consistently make the correct letter movement for each unjoined letter?					
Form letters without hesitation?					
Keep the pen or pencil on the paper for the whole letter movement?					
Make the correct join movement?					
Maintain the appropriate proportions for ascenders and short letters?					
Keep the pencil on the paper for the whole sequence of joined letters?					
Write joined sequences without hesitation?					

Name/Group: _____   Date: _____

Diagnostic assessment of handwriting

Copy the sentences quickly and neatly.

Foxes are nocturnal and omnivorous mammals.

There are twelve species of foxes, but the red fox is the most common.

In stories, foxes are often clever, bold, sly and quick.

Today, many red foxes in the UK prefer to live in towns, where there is plenty of rubbish to eat.

In your book, write three or four sentences about your dream holiday. Tell the reader where and when you would like to go, and what you would do there.

Write out the alphabet in lower-case letters. Write as quickly as you can, but make sure the letters are all readable.

Name/Group: _____   Date: _____

Speed and fluency practice sheet: Curly Caterpillar Letters

This sheet will help you to practise letters so you can write them automatically.

Write over then copy the letter pattern as quickly as you can.
Say the letter name as you write it.

ca ad

se fe

godg gdq

ecf ecf

qca qca

dfoq

qadf

caof

saeg

Happy Handwriting 5: Speed and fluency practice sheet: Curly Caterpillar Letters

Name/Group: _____   Date: _____

Speed and fluency practice sheet: Long Ladder Letters

This sheet will help you to practise letters so you can write them automatically.

Write over then copy the letter pattern as quickly as you can.
Say the letter name as you write it.

jyjy

kuku

ilil

ut ut

lukluk

iuk iuk

ytu ytu

iltk iltk

uytl uytl

jult jult

Name/Group: _____   Date: _____

Speed and fluency practice sheet: Robot and Zigzag Letters

This sheet will help you to practise letters so you can write them automatically.

*Write over then copy the letter pattern as quickly as you can.
Say the letter name as you write it.*

nm nm

rb rb

hm hm

bp bp

vnr vnr

wbn wbn

bhp bhp

rwm rwm

xhnr xhnr

zhmm zhmm

whnr whnr

Name/Group: _____   Date: _____

Extra practice sheet: diagonal joins

Warm up by continuing the pattern.

thethethe

Write a row of each of the prefixes.

pre   de
un   im

Add the prefixes above to the words below to make new words. Then write the new words.

___ possible

___ view

___ frost

___ believable

Copy the sentences.

It was impossible to catch the runaway dog.

Hamesh was inconsiderate when he finished all the cake.

How can making a decision be so unbelievably hard?

Name/Group: _____   Date: _____

Extra practice sheet: horizontal joins

Warm up by continuing the pattern.

rowrowrow

Write a row of each of the joins.

ure   ion

fr   on

Write over and copy out the words.

why

what

wherever

whenever

whose

Copy the sentences.

"It simply cannot be true!" exclaimed Rory.

Be careful because that water is poisonous.

The toughest competition is with yourself.

Name/Group: _____   Date: _____

Extra practice sheet: joins to round letters

Warm up by continuing the pattern.

cadcad

Write a row of each of the joins.

ed   ca

an   ic

Write over and then copy the words.

light

thought

calligraphy

heard

arctic

preferred

Copy the sentences.

Animals are not always friendly when they are tired.

The explorers managed to disturb the bears by making a noise.

Hibernating bears can run really fast.

Name/Group: _____   Date: _____

Extra practice sheet: capital letters for proper nouns

Fill in the missing capital letters.

A B C __ __ F G H __ __ K L __ N
O P __ __ S T __ __ W __ Y Z

Write out the letter sequences in capital letters.

lmno   bcde

pqrst   mnop

Correct the names by adding capital letters. Then copy the names into your book.

alicia   uncle raj

dr jones   ms sharensky

Correct the letter by adding capitals. Then copy it into your book.

max's Motor Cars
Racing road
warwick
cv44 9ds

dear mr kandula,

we would like to invite you to a special viewing of our vehicles. It will be on 30th march and will be opened by a top racing driver, mr mark speedy. Yours sincerely,

Bobby quick, Senior salesman

Guidance for alphabetical order tasks

Alphabet knowledge is one of the strongest predictors of reading success in young learners. Knowing the names of the letters allows us to talk about them and helps with phonics and spelling. It is very useful to be able to be clear when you mean the letter name c (pronounced *see*) or the sound /c/. If a child asks 'How do I spell /ch/ in 'chip'?', the answer 'using the letters c and h' is correct, but the answer 'with the sounds /c/ and /h/' is not. (These sounds do not blend to form /ch/.)

Learning letter names helps children to link lower-case and capital letters, too. Of course, it is also important to discuss the sounds associated with letters in phonics, and children have no difficulty learning both names and sounds.

Alphabetical order of letter names is an easily memorised sequence that lasts a lifetime. Later in children's education, this sequence helps them to use dictionaries, encyclopaedias and glossaries.

We hope all children will know the alphabet and letter names by Year 5. However, if you have children in the class who do not, we suggest you do the following to help them learn letter names and alphabetical order:

- Regularly sing the names of all the letters of the alphabet to a known tune. The most common tune is *Twinkle, Twinkle, Little Star*. Remember to name the last letter 'zed'. This is very important for children who join the class at this age.
- Use the alphabet cards (which can be printed out, laminated and cut up) to play games. Give each child a letter. (You may need some duplicates if there are more than 26 in the class.) Tell children that they need to jump up (or sit down) when their letter is sung, and then sing the alphabet song. You can adapt this activity so that children name an animal (for example) starting with their letter. Be mindful of children who may not be physically able to quickly sit and stand, and modify the game accordingly.
- As a class or group, do an alphabet hunt to create an alphabet list. Children take turns to find a word that begins with each letter of the alphabet, and the group leader writes up the list.
- Use the alphabetical order practice sheets to match up lower-case letters and capital letters.
- Use the alphabetical order practice sheets to make lists of items around the school, animals, and so on. The list of capital letters can be used to collect as many names (or place names) as possible.
- Hand out the alphabet cards when children need to line up for any sort of activity, so they can do it in alphabetical order. Children will soon start to recognise the section of the alphabet into which their letter falls. When the line is assembled, each child says the letter name on their card in turn.

Writing guidelines

Writing guidelines